www.BrooklynBooks.net

www.melodramapublishing.com

Library of Congress Control Number: 2017909430
ISBN-13: 978-1620780756
First Edition: November 2017

Printed in Canada

Crystal Lacey Winslow

Dedicated

To those formerly known as spendthrifts

"Debt is the slavery of the free"
– Publilius Syrus

Contents

Call to Order:

The Rules of the Cheap Girls Club

Welcome, cheap wannabes, to the first meeting of the Cheap Girls Club! Now, let's be honest, being called "cheap" isn't the typical girl's dream. But if being a cheap girl meant wealth, financial freedom, and a life without debt, would you be in?

Do you want that shop-till-you-drop, ball-out-of-control, first-class-seat type of money? No? Not you? How about that buy-your-dream-home, send-your-children-to-Ivy-League, retire-early type of cash flow? Whatever your money goals, your financial future begins and ends with accepting and embracing that you will get there quicker being cheap.

We all want what makes life easier: microwaveable dinners, laundry drop-off service, streaming movies, self-parking cars. To work smarter—not harder—should be everyone's goal. Whether you are a mom, entrepreneur, philanthropist, gold-digger, or socialite, money is a resource you must have, and the amount impacts your quality of life.

In 2015 the census estimated that 43.1 million Americans live in poverty. Crazy, right? Seems like a far cry from the American dream. Most people will never gross six-figures and could live three lifetimes and never net seven figures. That doesn't mean it isn't doable. If you make the right money choices, aim for financial literacy, and get on a trajectory toward debt freedom, you may find yourself in that sweet spot.

So why do we fail so miserably at managing our money? Why do we continually get into money trouble when there are so many tools and resources to help us spend wisely? There are so many cool things to indulge in, and sometimes living in the moment trumps the long haul. Sometimes the world of excessive living is too tempting and feels unavoidable. We feel we must partake or we'll miss out on the joys of life. But let's dig a little deeper, Cheap Girls.

The I's are the Why's:
Why People Get Into Money Trouble

Insecurity. Most of us have at least one thing we're insecure about. Sometimes these vulnerabilities trigger emotional spending. To make your life feel balanced, you splurge on items you don't need and often can't afford to make up for what you think you lack. The problem is you're just creating another imbalance—a financial imbalance.

When you are feeling insecure, your money will be devoted to things you cannot afford like designer clothes, designer shoes, luxury cars, and other big-ticket items in an attempt to boost your ego. With social media allowing people to "film and edit" their best lives, more people are ending up in debt trying to keep up with or impress their friends and followers.

Inflexibility. It starts as no fault. You get laid off, lose a second income due to divorce or separation, or suffer through a job demotion. The bottom line is there is a reduction in your finances. However, you do not adjust your lifestyle to match your current financial situation.

Imitation. A lot of us are our parents. If you witnessed your parents living paycheck to paycheck or living beyond their means, then you're predisposed to repeating that same toxic behavior.

In high school, right before we take out those massive college loans, we learn many things. Yet balancing a checkbook, staying out of debt, or saving for a rainy day is not on the curriculum. By the time you've graduated from college, you could already be six figures in arrears.

Indulgence. When you are kind-hearted, your generosity stems from an emotional draw to please—if not buy—other people. Before you even recognize the pattern, you spend most of your money (and your life) people-pleasing and indulging their whims. If buying someone's love is the cost to keep that person in your life, then that price is too high!

Whatever the "why," the result is still the same: debt. Don't beat yourself up. By picking up this book, you've made the first step. Your economic U-turn has just begun. I can admit I've lived through it all—the dark, gloomy hole of debt, buying things to project wealth, and, regretfully, buying love. Listen, trying to keep up with the Kardashians is foolish, and cheap girls are smart girls. That's why the Cheap Girls Club mission is to teach you to make wise financial decisions as women. So let's get this cheap party started!

Cheap Girls on a Mission

Your mission, should you accept it, is to save more and spend less to invest! Become your own financial advisor, watch your money grow, and become a full-fledged cheapskate.

Now let's go over the rules to transform you into a fearless, unapologetic Cheap Girl.

15 Rules for the Cheap Girls Club:

1. No obsessing or stewing over spilled milk. If the money is gone, you can always make it back. That's how winners think.

2. Stop complaining. No one wants to hear you always whining about being broke. People will distance themselves from you because, ultimately, people feel being broke is contagious.

3. Think and dream big. We attract what we believe. If you keep thinking about being in debt, it will be that much harder for you to dig yourself out. What's the best possible scenario for you? Close your eyes and envision you are debt-free. What does that look like for you? Connect to the emotions. How do you feel? Awesome, right?

4. It's not over until it's over. Unless you're dead, you can always make a comeback. How many games have you watched where the losing team came back to win in the ninth inning?

5. Get your grind on. Abraham Lincoln said that the good things that happen to those who wait are only the things left behind by those who hustle. If our sixteenth president was hustling in the nineteenth century, then what are you doing?

6. "No" shall become the first, second, third, and default word you will speak to yourself and others. Learn it. Live it. Like it. Love it. Boom!

7. Think cheap. Being cheap is an art form, and you are the artist. *Cheap* shall become your mantra, motto, and maxim. Master your craft, because cheap is the new black.

8. Respect money. You respect yourself, your parents, and people in authority. Stop disrespecting your money by throwing it away on worthless things that don't serve you or your goals.

Cut it out. It's stupid!

9. Do your homework. Not everyone learns about money and finance through osmosis. Educating yourself is invaluable.

10. Sweat *all* bills—even the small ones.

11. Gradually go full-blown cheapskate. Yeah, that's a rule. This won't happen in the blink of an eye, but small changes over time will put a huge dent in your transformation.

12. Commit. If you're not all the way in, how can your money follow suit? Commit to the Cheap Girls Club and win!

13. Let fear motivate you. Let the fear of losing it all spark a fire in you. Just as Popeye has his spinach, use your fear to strengthen your will to be cheap.

14. Self-control is your anti-broke mechanism. Master it.

15. You will hold yourself and yourself alone accountable for any bad financial decisions.

This book is divided into three parts:

Part One

The first section will walk you through simple steps to save money on everyday essentials. It will help you identify areas where you are overspending and give you tips to cut costs and save more toward your goal of financial freedom.

Part Two

Part two focuses on how to stack the money you are now saving and change the way you look at money. This section will help you identify your spending triggers, pinpoint where your money is unnecessarily flowing and why. Is your bleak financial situation predicated on your wants or the needs of others? This section should reel you back in. You will learn steps on how to go on a spending diet without feeling starved. If you change the way you think about the money you earn, save, and invest, then you change your future.

Part Three

The third section outlines options for investing the saved money into your retirement, at whatever age.

Introduction

And so it began …

*Y*ou're cheap!"

As a kid, that was never how I wanted to be defined, nor how I saw myself. The negative undertone instantly made me feel unlikable. I was maybe ten or eleven years old. I would save all my holiday cash and chore money in my Pinocchio savings bank for that one big-ticket item I'd been eyeing. My two siblings, who had blown through their money, would come sniffing around for my cash. I would object, and I was called "cheap." The look of contempt on their faces—deep frowns coupled with resentment—made me feel guilty, like I should share what I had earned and saved. My ability to save at such a young age was compartmentalized into that one word. "Cheap." Seeing I was outnumbered by my two teen siblings, my dad intervened and said, "She's not cheap; she's thrifty."

I did not understand what that word meant, nor did being described as "thrifty" make me feel any better. But he was right, my dad. I was thrifty. I wasn't a selfish child. I just wanted to save my money so I could purchase the desires of my young heart. The distinguishable wordplay was too minor to matter. Being cheap, thrifty, or frugal are often interchangeable, subjective, and, frankly, relative. All those words left a bad taste in my mouth, and I buckled under the pressure.

Whenever my siblings decided they wanted my saved money for frivolous things like snacks from the corner store (we're not talking major bucks here), I would reluctantly give it up to appease them. It took ages to get to the origin of my money issues, but I realized that a psychosomatic transformation had taken root. Always bullied about being cheap, I settled into a routine that would haunt me for years to come.

Part 1

Save More

Chapter One

Define: Cheap

So what does it mean to go cheap? *Cheap* has an off-putting nuance because it's been touted in the worst ways—to justify petty behavior. I have met a lot of cheap *and* petty people in my life. Those people don't represent the Cheap Girls Club. That's not what we embody. Fundamentally, this movement is all about being cheap *and* principled—classy-cheap, not petty-cheap.

Do you have the soul of a moocher? Do you consistently manipulate do-gooders to pick up the tab? Are you that girl who feels that your money is yours and others' money is yours? We all know that one person who undoubtedly will suck the air out of a room by being cheap in a petty way. The girl with that "if-it's-free-then-it's-my-kinda *par-tay* attitude" understands it's not free. She knows someone had to pay for it, and she doesn't care.

Cheap means different things to different people. Essentially, what our kind of cheap is *not* is taking advantage of people and manipulating systems for those truly in need. The petty-cheap plot and scheme, and ultimately use those around them. It's only about receiving. They breeze through life never wanting to pay their fair share. They feel the world owes them something never understanding that they are owed nothing.

Looting the condiments at your local fast-food franchise because you refuse to purchase your own supply is not my kind of cheap. Stealing cable, pirating movies, or tricking a kind-hearted person into picking up the tab is not what the Cheap Girls Club is about.

Showing up to a party or gathering empty-handed and lying to the host that you plan to get them a gift later is uncouth. Have some tact. Petty-cheap people go too far. They have no etiquette. Petty is an irritating trait, and some individuals have been sharpening this skill for years.

I recently watched a courtroom reality show where the plaintiff was suing her landlord for theft of property. She had a laundry list of expensive items she wanted to be reimbursed for, including a two-thousand-dollar front loading washer, a four-thousand-dollar Samsung refrigerator with a television in the door, and a six-thousand-dollar Wolf range. The list totaled over thirty thousand dollars' worth of appliances. The plaintiff spoke well, was well dressed, and had on flashy jewelry. But here's the kicker—this grown woman was in a program that paid 100% of her rent. Not a percentage, not a one-time deal because she fell on hard times, but her full $2,200 per month rent was being paid with our tax dollars. Wait, what?

The judge was astonished by the plaintiff's high-end amenities. As she proudly boasted that she "liked nice things," the judge couldn't help but quip, "Yeah, so do I. But I also can pay my own rent."

See, this is one example of petty-cheap. People, as a profession, manipulate the programs that should be reserved for disadvantaged individuals. These programs are being abused, and it hurts everyone. I repeat: petty-cheap people do an injustice to us all.

Years ago, seven of my friends and I went out to dinner at a favorite Brooklyn restaurant. I had invited my BFF, Rory, who is excruciatingly petty-cheap. It's who she is, and she will be no one other than her authentic self. The bill came, and with a healthy tip, it meant that we would pony up a measly $60 each. We dipped in our wallets and placed our shares at the center of the table, only to tally up the cash and come up exactly $60 short. One person didn't contribute. Instinctively, all heads turned toward her. The whole time Rory was ordering crab legs and steak and tossing back fruity cocktails, she knew she would eat for free. "Let the suckers pick up my tab" was her lifelong mantra. Instantly, my stomach became queasy because I knew two things: I knew that she didn't pay, and I also knew that when she was caught doing petty, she got loud.

She began with, "I did so pay! I pulled out three twenties, right? You saw me, right?"—She looked to me to cosign. I remained quiet.

Everyone at the table had witnessed each person dropping their money, except her. She continued to scream, which brought forth our waitress. Politely she asked us if everything was OK. At that point I reached into my wallet again and pulled out an additional $60 to cover my friend's tab. However, my other six friends would not allow me to take the full loss. The seven of us covered the missing $60. Guess who wouldn't contribute one dollar toward the missing money? Obviously, the petty-cheap friend.

That scenario reminded me of the Bible parable when two women fight over a baby, and the wise King Solomon threatens to cut the baby in half. One woman says, "Go ahead," feeling no remorse that the baby will be killed, while the child's real mother begs the king not to kill her baby. Therefore, she was declared the child's actual mother.

The people at the table who reached into their pockets to settle the additional debt were the same people who contributed to the original bill. This was one of many teachable moments. Rory is a few years my senior, and I learned a lot from her. I discovered the person I never wanted to become.

Takers gravitate toward givers. It balances the universe. Now had I been a petty-cheap person, Rory and I would have continually clashed.

I tell ya, I use to despise that word *cheap*. From the first time my sisters called me out, I didn't want its stink on me. But I've grown, I've learned, and I now find beauty in the word. Cheap is allowing me to sleep peacefully at night, live debt-free, and focus on retirement. Cheap people respect money and know to invest it so it goes to work for them. To go cheap means to think before you buy, only spend what you've earned, and never buy anything full price. It doesn't mean being petty, manipulative, or preying on the givers.

If you are inherently petty-cheap, this book won't help you much. You will not learn new ways to reap without sowing. Join the club because you are searching for a financial awakening. Join the club to tap into unchartered territory. Join the club to establish economic boundaries.

🕐 Meditative Minutes

I know you may be tempted to jump all in to this club and focus on ways to save, recoup lost earnings, or make up for lost time. However, note that it all can be done with grace. Don't allow parasitic behavior to overshadow your principles. Take a few minutes to meditate on the classy-cheap girl you are.

Cheap Girls Club Oath

We can often be influenced by those around us. There's a saying, a girl who socializes with smart friends is smart. Don't allow the petty-cheap people of the world to hijack your principles. Their methods can be a seduction that may be hard to resist, especially if you're a newbie to the club. Purge their teachings and start from scratch using the Cheap Girls Club rules. As you embark on this journey, make a mental note that *how* you save more matters.

Chapter Two

You've Found Yourself in Debt. Now What?

The first time I met debt's acquaintance, I was nineteen years old, in my first year in college, and living with my boyfriend. Things were rocky in my relationship, so for spring break I visited family in Virginia. The first day I arrived, I rented a mid-size car. Because of my age, I had to add a secondary driver, which I did. However, I was emphatic that the co-driver, my cousin Marie, would not have driving privileges.

I will never forget when the valet brought out a Mazda 929, gold with tan leather seats. Less than one hundred miles was on this car, and I could smell the newness. The Virginia weather was all sunny skies and warm breezes. I opened the sunroof and smoothly peeled out of the car lot, excited about my much-needed vacation.

That night was uneventful. I settled in with family and made plans to hang out with my best friend the next day. I remember going to bed early, leaving a full house downstairs. Around seven the next morning, I was awakened to the news that my car key was stolen and the brand-new Mazda 929 was totaled. Latoya, a friend of Marie's, had gone for a joy ride with my rented wheels and smashed into a light pole.

Since Latoya wasn't a licensed driver, she used Marie's name, which was on the rental agreement. The police looked up Marie's name and address and dropped Latoya off to the residence to make sure she was who she said she was. All this was taking place while I was upstairs counting sheep. Marie went to the front door and realized that her friend used her name, there would be an infraction on her license, and that she would also be on the hook to pay for damaging the street light. What did my cousin do? Well, the right thing. Marie told the police that her friend had falsely used her name, and Latoya was promptly arrested.

I'll never forget arriving at the car rental lot and seeing the Mazda twisted. The car looked like crumbled paper. The coldness from the rental staff couldn't compare to how numb I felt. This was all too much. A myriad of emotions and thoughts overwhelmed me. I was confused, I was angry, and sadly, I felt alone. I was alone. It was only my name to take responsibility for that contract. And if I thought I had covered all my bases when I bought insurance coverage, well, I was rocked yet again. The rental car company worked fast. They had a copy of the police report naming a driver (Latoya) that wasn't on my agreement, so at this moment I wasn't covered. Frantically I explained that the car was stolen by the named driver. I was asked if I had filed a police report for theft, and I hadn't, since I had only found out about the incident a couple hours earlier.

I went back to my family's home and called the sheriff's office to make a formal report of theft. When they arrived, they found two bickering women with conflicting stories. See, Marie, who had done the right thing and sent her friend to jail when her name was on the line, suddenly felt that sending that same friend to jail for stealing a car was unconscionable.

Marie had absolutely no idea of what I would have to endure because of her lie. Under the policy, if I willingly gave the key to someone who was not listed under the coverage, then I was not insured. The insurance company had three statements, two saying that I had willingly given the key to the unlicensed, uninsured driver, and my story—that the key was stolen while I was asleep. I was outnumbered, and this allowed the insurance company to deny my claim. I was dejected. It was an overwhelming experience for someone my age to bear, and there I was, in another state, helpless.

Back in New York, it was hard to concentrate on my classes. I was bombarded with threatening letters and phone calls. Angry collectors inundated my headspace. The demand was ten thousand dollars down, and twenty-five dollars a month after that until the debt was paid. This was exorbitant for most, and astronomical for a second-semester college student. Immediately, I hired an attorney to fight for me. For five hundred dollars he made a few calls and reviewed the rental agreement, but ultimately, I was held liable. Although this was the first time I had incurred debt, it would not be the last. I had vowed to be a responsible adult. I had instability in my childhood that I had no control over, but college would be a new beginning. Or so I had hoped.

Less than a year later, a judgment totaling over fifty thousand dollars had my name on it. The blue book value for the car, attorney fees, and court costs plus interest was awarded to the rental company. Rightfully so—someone had to pay, and the car rental company shouldn't have been left holding the bag. But this was a situation where I had done my part. Which is all I could have done, other than being more mindful of the company I kept.

From that moment, I was on a trajectory toward self-destruction. I bought things to lessen the pain, gobbling up everything my preexisting credit cards had room for. Then the bottom fell out. I was drowning in old and new debt. I desperately wanted to click my heels three times and wish the situation away. But I could not. I would eventually have to face reality. Until then, it followed me around like a menacing pit bull, dictating what I could and could not do.

So there I was, a broke full-time student, working part-time. This was a sizable debt, and to say I wasn't ready is an understatement. Having that massive judgment on all three credit reports cost me a lot. Besides not being able to apply for new credit—credit cards, school loans, car loans, or any apartments in my name—my credit score was in the toilet. And there would be a long road ahead of me to clean up the mess.

A year after I graduated with my bachelor's degree, I had a full-time job in my field. The new position came with a fifteen-thousand-dollar pay increase, and I saved the additional income for a dream of mine. I secretly had big plans of opening a laundromat, which took a lot of capital.

During that period, I was working at a law firm, and although my name was in the company directory, my telephone number was incorrectly listed. I was embarrassed when a managing attorney came to advise me she was receiving numerous calls from a collection agent. The debt lingered in the back of my mind, but honestly, I tried to forget it. When I thought about it, my heart would palpitate and I'd feel lightheaded and short of breath. I knew I had to handle this situation, but when you're making forty thousand a year, you can't fathom paying out fifty.

The collection agent was relentless. Although I gave her my correct number, she continued to call my manager and leave messages and call the operator to connect us. Her strong-arm tactic worked, and I negotiated a settlement and promptly paid the debt. I just wanted the ordeal to finally be put behind me. The settlement took all my savings and then some, quelled my vision of owning and operating my own business, and put me back in the poorhouse. In my early twenties, I already needed my financial life back.

I know how it feels to max out all your credit cards, to have more rent due than money earned, and to come home to an eviction notice taped to your front door for all your neighbors to see. I know how it feels to have hunger pains, to consistently open the refrigerator knowing there isn't any food in it. I know how the words feel tumbling out of your mouth to ask family to loan you a few dollars only to be told that they're struggling too. I had bounced back from debt so many times until I asked myself, "You're in debt. Now what?"

That black hole you've found yourself in that seemingly is sucking all the air out your lungs feels overwhelming, I know. But it's not. It's a problem, and problems are solvable. You must kill money anxiety by knowing there's a way out. Look around, and you might realize that you are not alone. Most people have been worried sick about money. Ask yourself what are you *legally* willing to do to get debt-free? It's like this: you must put out an equal force to come out even, and a greater force to get ahead. You can slowly chip away at debt while interest and/or penalties keep accruing, or you can go hard and show debt who's boss.

The road to debt is usually unremarkable. Have you ever asked yourself where your money went? What did you spend it on? You look around, and there isn't anything to show for those high credit card bills or depleted savings account. Before you know it, you've accumulated too many expenses.

In 2008, Americans went through a recession. It lasted a couple years for some, and it is still unraveling for others. Home foreclosures, unemployment, and insurmountable credit card debt left people insecure about their futures. People are still, a decade later, trying to regain solid financial footing. All this financial stress could lead to depression. An economic depression isn't an isolated condition. It's an epidemic. It's worldwide, and every income class is susceptible.

Debt is not a poor person's problem. I repeat. This is not a poor person's problem. Millionaires have money problems—billionaires, too. Remember the MC Hammer story? The "U Can't Touch This" and "2 Legit 2 Quit" artist, multi-millionaire, and icon, who filed Chapter 11 bankruptcy at the height of his career? Hammer, who built his dream home for $12 million and ultimately sold it for $5.3, allegedly went into debt spending lavishly and supporting family and friends. I know it not only feels better to give than to receive, but it's also a mantra often repeated. It's deceitful. Yes, be generous, but choose wisely who benefits from your charitable heart. Since 2015, my mantra has been: I'll see your "it's better to give than to receive" and raise you "no good deed goes unpunished."

Sometimes debt comes unexpectedly, like a thief in the night. You're on vacation and get bitten by an infected mosquito. Or you're traveling and get injured. You're uninsured, and you rack up medical bills and lose everything. Maybe debt came in a frenzy. You go on an impromptu shopping spree or got suckered into a timeshare vacation club. It could come through a friend. You want to help out your sister-friend, and you get stuck paying her debt.

How many people will go on vacation, stay with family at what they feel is a safe haven, and go home with over fifty thousand dollars in debt? Not many. I've dissected this situation a hundred times. What could I have done differently? The answer is a resounding *nothing*. Evidently, I was to learn the "shit happens" lesson early.

Listen, if we dwell in the "why me" space, we will never move forward. Now, it's easy for me to say brush it off your shoulders, but back then it felt like the walls were closing in on me. I firmly believe that our lives are preordained, and that everything that is supposed to happen will. Each event, like breadcrumbs, leads you closer to monumental events, good and bad. You must take both journeys, no shortcuts.

We've all heard that life isn't fair. Amen. But debt is always earned—directly or indirectly. I gained that fifty-thousand-dollar debt through my stupidity. Accountability is essential. I fell asleep in a house full of people who weren't on my team and left something of value unprotected. Today the movement is Stay Woke. This

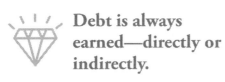

Debt is always earned—directly or indirectly.

is a cautionary tale of getting caught sleeping and ending up in a pile of debt! The takeaway is be careful of who you let in your inner circle, family included. When I ask the question, "How many people are in debt for family and friends?" the number goes up exponentially. Think about that.

After taking a long look at my journey, I realized that I had to hold myself accountable for my past, present, and future financial decisions. Debt came gift-wrapped with a bow of unpredictability. But isn't that life?

Even with the major setbacks of debt, I own and operate two companies, own several investment properties (rental and commercial), have a diverse investment portfolio with profitable gains, cash assets, make maximum contributions into my self-funded pension plan, healthcare coverage, vacation abroad yearly, am 100% debt-free, and living my best life with purpose and clarity as a Cheap Girl. Not bad for a high-school dropout, huh?

In the beginning stages, the early realization that your bills have piled up can evoke so many emotions: panic, shock, anger, anxiety, denial, depression, and fear. Momentarily, step away. Remember, gradual is the name of the game. Below are a few dos and don'ts for when the reality bomb first drops.

Do:

◊ Have a realistic outlook on your financial situation.
◊ Gather literature (such as this book) on financial awareness. Read, study, implement.
◊ Create a budget.
◊ Execute a Payback Plan.

Don't:

◊ Don't do any financial planning until you've sifted through your emotions. Nothing will get accomplished until you are level-headed.
◊ Don't create new debt to suppress the off-putting feelings of old debt.
◊ Don't get discouraged.
◊ Don't make excuses. Put in the work.

Meditative Minutes

We've found ourselves in debt, and that debt-monster might appear undefeatable. It's not. Take a few minutes to meditate and quiet your restless mind. Close your eyes, clear your mind, and allow all negative thoughts to wash away. Breathe in (through your nose) the worry, angst, and all the uncomfortable feelings that go with debt. And then release (through your mouth). Let it all go.

Cheap Girls Club Oath

Some will argue that because I can recall the rental car situation that I am bitter or holding on to the past. But neither of those is true. I am a writer, and that's what we do. We write about experiences we've had—pleasant and unpleasant—or would like to have. Although my cousin never asked for forgiveness nor apologized for being a co-conspirator, I forgave her a long time ago. I just didn't forget. *Never* forget a good lesson. Never forget something as powerful as a teachable moment.

After this incident, I can't count how often grown women have asked me if I could rent a car or rent an apartment in my name for them. Just as listed at rule #6, I spew, "NO." I can't explain how annoyed and angry people can get when turned down. See, these people are one situation too late. I have already been scorched by the hot pot. I survived an inferno and am not willing to place my credit history and peace of mind at risk for anyone else, ever. Instead of allowing my credit to suffer in someone else's hands, I became a Cheap Girl. Take the oath with me. When your name, finances, or good credit are asked to be put on the line for someone—anyone—just say **NO**. You're in the Cheap Girls Club, and NO is our way of life.

Chapter Three

Ways to Save:
Tips and Tricks to Save More Money

I used to be a sucker for a sale. Something about saving money tapped into the child I was, and spending it enticed the woman I turned out to be. I thought that by spending money, I was saving it. I didn't realize that if I saved five bucks on a ten-dollar item I did not need, I didn't gain five dollars. I lost five. Half-price items seduced me directly to the poorhouse. Although I didn't have any money, I had lots of stuff to go around.

The sobering truth is that stuff can't pay your rent. I had so much stuff there was a time when my family called me a hoarder. Not in the messy, fire-hazard sense of the word, but because I was excessive. Before *The Walking Dead*, I was stocking my fridge and pantry for a zombie apocalypse. If you walked into my home, the storage closets, kitchen cabinets,

The sobering truth is that stuff can't pay your rent.

and drawers were all stocked with dozens and dozens of items I didn't need or couldn't use before their expiration dates. Week after week, if I wasn't tossing unopened dairy, produce, or meats into the trash, then someone was using my home to shop for their own essentials—paper towels, shampoo, cleaning supplies, the works. Oh, I was happy to give these items away because I had gotten them "on sale," and these items would just "go to waste," right?

I was a fool. Though I was obsessed with saving money, I was doing the complete opposite. By trying to save money, I was actually losing it. Once I recognized this pattern, it was too late. My spending was out of control, my credit cards were maxed out, and I couldn't walk past a sale or discount without making a purchase. It was insane. Stocking up on these items made me feel, well, better—like I had a security blanket. I snuggled up with ski suits I would never use and two mountain bikes I would never ride. Honestly, I purchased the two bikes simultaneously because they were discounted and I couldn't decide on a color.

The tips in this chapter are about how to save money on needs, not wants. Each day we must fight off frivolous spending. With so much temptation, it gets hard to resist the wants. If you want what you want when you want it, here are ways you can get it at a reduced cost. In Part Two of *Cheap Girls Club*, you'll learn tips to not want it at all.

Everyday Ways To Save

Most people don't look for the means to save until they already have one foot firmly planted in debt. They're scrambling, panicking, and trying to negotiate with companies when they don't have the upper hand. It's easier to negotiate from a position of power. The best time to discuss lowering interest rates, the benefits of

It's easier to negotiate from a position of power.

having A+ credit, and getting things gratis is when you are a valuable consumer. Each year you must look for discounts. Don't get the home security system after your home has been broken into. Use preemptive measures to keep bills down.

Lower Your Monthly Bills

Cancel Your Cable

I remember years back, I went to England to visit a friend. Home after home had no television. When I asked why, I thought the English response would be filled with stuffy sarcasm—that I'd hear, "We don't watch television in England, we read." Instead, they explained that they just refused to pay for cable. That was twelve years ago, and they were on to something. Nowadays more families are cutting the cable cord and saving a considerable amount of money. Ask yourself this. Does the three-in-one telephone, television, and Internet package with the introductory rate of $99.99 plus tax have value? Before you realize it, your bill is over two hundred dollars a month, your home phone is only good for robocalls, and you watch maybe five out of the hundreds of channels you are paying for. If your cell phone is your primary form of verbal communication, then do you need the home line? Do you watch those premium channels? So that leaves the Internet. Here are some viable Internet-based programming options:

You can purchase an antenna. Most new-model televisions make connectivity relatively easy for broadcast television networks. You can get at least forty free channels and save upwards of $2400 a year. If you own a smart TV, then you can watch Crackle, a free streaming service with hundreds of uninterrupted movies and television series. If not, then you can get a streaming device such as Roku, which lets you stream networks directly to your television.

You can keep only the Internet and add a service like Netflix if you want to broaden your viewing selection. For even more bang for your buck, you can get the premium plan and share costs.

If you're an Amazon aficionado, then Amazon Prime's streaming service is something to consider. The yearly membership fee pays for itself by offering free shipping on all purchases and their streaming service.

You can get a casting device, like a Chromecast ($35), which allows you to stream free live events and videos from services like YouTube directly to your TV from your phone or Chrome web browser. You might be surprised by how much content you can cast for free.

Gas Bills

Stay away from fixed monthly bills. This is a luxury option at a premium price. The gas company loves to send you letters on how you can pay the same bill each month to help you balance your checkbook. What they won't tell you is that your "fixed" rate is at the highest price per therm. I fell into this trap. When gas prices were at 56¢ per therm, I was paying $1.07. Unknowingly, I did this for two years.

To save money on your gas bill, the simplest solution is a programmable thermostat. During winter months the utility department advises to set it to 72 degrees during the evening. Overnight, the thermostat should drop to 67 degrees. However, this advice is contingent on your comfort level, but if you follow the experts' advice, then you'll save a considerable amount of money.

*Bonus Tip: Using a toaster oven saves money on your gas bill. Instead of firing up that large gas oven to make your children spring rolls or chicken nuggets, a small energy-efficient toaster oven does the same job at a fraction of the cost.

Electric Bills:

If you haven't done so already, go through your home and replace all your light bulbs with energy-efficient lighting. LED bulbs are a good place to start. They last up to 25 times longer than incandescent bulbs and use 75% less energy. Unplug all power guzzlers when you aren't using them (coffee makers, X-box games, DVD players). Set your outdoor lighting to programmable dusk/dawn settings or use solar-powered lights. Always buy energy-efficient appliances and shut lights off when not in use.

Free Energy Monitoring Apps

◊ Lightbulbfinder.net has an app that helps individuals locate bulbs that help save money and energy.
◊ MyMeter
◊ Energy CURB

Trash Pickup

If you're a homeowner and have to pay for trash pickup, don't get lax. If your bill is steadily rising, first call competing companies to see what their rates are and then call your company to see if you can negotiate a better deal. Should your company not play ball and lower your price, you'll be able to make a well-informed decision to switch.

Water Bills

Be mindful. Don't allow the water to run while brushing your teeth, don't let the shower run for extended periods of time before you get in, and don't allow your sprinkler system to "over-water" your lawn.

For a few bucks at your local home improvement store purchase a high-efficiency, faucet aerator. These smart devices help save money on water and energy.

Most homeowners shy away from using their dishwasher because of the perceived cost. However, if you have an energy-efficient dishwasher, you conserve more water using it than you would washing by hand.

Cell Phone

The days of paying high mobile phone bills should be in your past. Verizon has a customer loyalty plan that's good. T-Mobile and Sprint offer services where additional lines are minimal. A family of four with unlimited data could spend roughly $25 - $30 per line on T-Mobile. Sprint has a competitive offer. Look for the best plan with unlimited data, autopay discount, and family vs. individual plans. Shop around and don't lock yourself into long-term contracts.

Alarm System

I used to think that all alarm systems were different and often went with the most recognizable brand to protect my home. However, all systems have a central station. Once an alarm signal is received, they contact authorities if they're unable to reach the homeowner. Shop around and you'll be surprised that a lot of companies offer free installation and keypad(s), and are at least 30% less expensive than the name brand company.

Insulation

This is a rare tip where you have to spend money to save it. If you're a homeowner with drafty rooms and heat loss, you might want to add adequate insulation. You can reduce your energy bills by adding rolled, batt, or expand-in-place insulation, blow-in fibers, rigid boards, or pour-in insulation to your attic. It's a cost-effective way to save.

There are so many obvious leaks in many households that can be addressed to help save energy, and money. You can buy weather stripping to add to your windows and doors even if both are new. And energy efficient companies come out for a fee.

Also, there may be energy-efficient federal tax credits available. These credits do not apply to labor costs.

◊ https://www.irs.gov/uac/form-5695-residential-energy-credits

Windows

If you do not have the budget to replace all your windows with energy-efficient ones, then you can use pre-cut insulation shrink sheets, spray foams and weather stripping to seal up drafts and gaps. Heavier drapes also help reduce draft during the winter months and keep your home cooled down during the summer months.

Memberships

Gym

Unless you're a gymnast training for Pyeongchang or a triathlete competing in a triathlon, I frown upon such memberships. If you are looking to save more and spend less, I would place gym membership in the "cancel" column. This extravagance is an unnecessary drain on your finances when there are so many free options available. Should everyone concentrate on self-care? Absolutely. However, there are many free exercises such as walking, jogging, lunges, yoga, calisthenics. You can purchase a trampoline or free weights from any discount store, and you can even use something as basic as a chair to whip your body into shape.

Warehouse Club Costs

The first time I walked into Costco it was: Mind. Blown. The shopaholic in me went berserk. The $55 price tag for a membership seemed reasonable. And then I got to the counter, and my cart was four or five times more than I would have spent at my local market.

Costco, Sam's Club, and BJ's have popped up, and I've dabbled in them all. Here's my take. Everything under the umbrella of these bargain stores is not a bargain. You can find lower prices elsewhere, including local dollar stores. Couple that with the yearly fee, and you could actually lose money. What determines value is how many people are in your household, how often you go there to shop, and distance. These warehouse clubs are ideal for large families, and patrons who split the membership cost.

Fees

Credit Card APR (Annual Percentage Rate)

Credit Card APR is the silent killer. If you pay your credit card each month, then you avoid the interest rate altogether. Sometimes that's impossible. Before you get into a situation where you're paying high interest rates, call your credit card providers to lower your APR. If you're carrying a high balance and they refuse to lower your rate, an option would be to transfer the balance to a card with a lower APR. Some cards offer zero introductory transfer rates. For instance, if you have a card with a balance of $1000, and the APR is 28.9%, and another card is offering 0% on the transferred balance and APR for 18 months. You transfer the balance and pay it off within that time frame because after 18 months the balance will jump to a higher rate.

Checking Account Fees

If you're paying checking account fees each month, you should be working on getting an account that offers free checking. Some require a minimum balance in order to remain free, so make sure your account doesn't fall below that threshold.

ATM Fees

Never pay an ATM fee. When I was younger, I was careless and would pull fast-cash out of the nearest ATM. I would get hit regularly, and those fees quickly ate away at my savings. Only use an ATM of your credit union or bank, or use your debit card to get cash back to avoid fees. At $3.00 per transaction, if you use another financial institution's ATM twice a week you will spend more than $300 per year in fees.

Rewards and Free Money

Pay off your credit cards each month in full to take advantage of your rewards—cash back, airline miles, and reward points.

Cash Bonuses

There are loads of incentives with banks that offer rewards such as setting up direct deposit or depositing a specific amount of dollars and earning up to $500.00 in bonus money. The fine print reads that you can't get both offers, so be certain to choose the most money. For example, setting up direct deposit could earn you $200, and, as an example, a $1500 deposit could make $300. If the $1500 earns you more, then go with that. I know this seems self-explanatory, but the promotions are misleading. The fine print will give you the lesser of the two bonuses.

Flight and Hotel Rewards

If you're in good credit standing and not swimming in debt, several reward cards have real incentive. Should you already be in debt, then don't tempt yourself with more. A lot of credit card companies have partnered with airlines and hotel chains. If you apply, you could earn 25,000 introductory points to an airline. Depending on the carrier, most domestic flights are 25,000 points or less. For example, American Express has a Delta credit card. Citibank has partnered with American Airlines and Hilton, and Chase has linked up with United Airlines.

Reward Points

Each year, around November, some credit cards offer discounts on their reward catalogue. Look for these savings before Black Friday. If an iPad is usually 120,000 points, it might be lowered to 85,000 points—a good deal. If your points don't expire, get the biggest bang for your buck by allowing your points to accumulate. Look for electronics— flat-screen televisions is my reward of choice.

Cash Back Rewards

If you are serious about saving more, and you also have an understanding of money, credit cards that offer cash back are smart. Should you have this option, then instead of using your debit card, place all your recurring bills on your credit. Use your checking account to pay the credit cards off in full so as to not incur APR fees and place payments on autopay. Before placing your reoccurring bills on your credit card set up bill alerts to track how much is due. For instance, most companies will send you a courtesy email or text alert before the bill's due date. Therefore, you can balance your checkbook and there won't be any surprises when the credit card bill is due. Chapter Seven has apps that can help. Make cards with this option work for you. Cash back is usually in reward dollars and will be issued as a statement credit.

Please note: Some credit cards have an annual fee. Read each Card Agreement, and decide which is best for you and your family.

◊ **Chase Freedom** offers 5% cash back up to $1500 and 1% thereafter.

◊ **Blue Cash Preferred®** card from American Express offers 6% cash back up to $6000.

◊ **Discover it®** - Cashback Match™ offers 5% cash back on rotating categories and 1% cash back (unlimited) on all other purchases.

Fuel

There are a couple ways to save on gas. Some supermarket reward cards offer discounts on fuel if you spend a certain amount each month. For instance, Kroger (you can also use your fuel points at Shell) gives you points for shopping at their store. For every $100 you spend that month, you can redeem your points for up to 10 cents off each gallon. So if you spend $200, you get 20 cents off per gallon. And 3 cents off each gallon even if you make no purchases. Some credit cards offer double points on fuel. Whatever you do, don't open a new credit card to save on gas.

Reward Websites

◊ **Ebates:** This is basically an affiliate program. You sign up, make purchases from the site from over 2000 specific stores and earn up to 40% cash back. You also get referral fees. There is a cap on how much you can earn; everything is in the fine print. This is a good way to earn extra cash on everyday purchases.

◊ **Swagbucks:** Such a cute name. This affiliate program has the same infrastructure but the rewards differ slightly. This site offers cash and gift cards when you complete online surveys, watch movie trailers, and try special offers. Again, a good way to earn extra money toward financial freedom.

Full Price

Never, ever, and I repeat, ever, pay full price for anything. Even food.

Clothing

If I know one thing, I know clothing. I also know that if you want to save money, don't buy cheaply made clothes. Cheap Girls do not wear cheaply made garments, as they will cost you more eventually. You can spend $40.00 on a cheap dress from a cheap store that won't last a season. You can get quality, high-end, trendy clothing on sale for the same price, and it will last you for years. Once you become a pro at sniffing out sales, you can find a three-hundred-dollar dress for a fraction of the price. If you want to be fashion forward with a 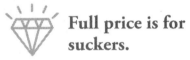 **Full price is for suckers.** limited budget, buy clothes that are multi-functioning from outlets. Saks OFF 5TH, Nordstrom Rack, Neiman Marcus' Last Call, T.J.Maxx, Ross Stores, Marshalls, and DSW for shoes are great places to start. Two out of three Americans shop at outlets for better deals. However, always comparison-shop and take time to peruse clearance items for even steeper discounts. Remember to check your price comparison apps, set a budget, and don't overspend. For clothing, cheap means inexpensively purchased.

Furnishings

HomeGoods, T.J.Maxx, and Marshalls have an extensive selection of interior items. You can find things from six-piece dining room sets to high thread-count sheets, stemware, and outdoor furnishings. Cheap Girls do not pay full price on anything, including furniture.

Thrift Stores

I used to cringe at the thought of shopping thrift. That whole "previous owner" thing gave me the creeps. And then there's the aspect of hygiene. Nowadays, I love thrifting and antiquing. A hobby of mine is upcycling—repurposing items instead of trashing them. It helps save our planet and lessens my carbon blueprint. You can find mostly anything in a thrift store. You will be amazed at what you could buy for ten bucks or less. Locate a good thrift store in your area and watch the savings pour in.

Vehicles

Car lots such as CarMax offer large selections of used vehicles. I start there because vehicles aren't appreciating assets, and the moment you drive a new car off the lot it depreciates. A used car is a fiscally responsible choice, but don't purchase one that's too old because of the potential for costly

Vehicles aren't appreciating assets.

repairs. Three to five years old is a good start. If you absolutely MUST purchase a new car, the best time to shop is September. Salespeople are looking to clear out inventory for the upcoming model year and to hike up their quarter-end numbers. Also, be mindful of what it will cost to insure your car. People often overlook that.

Taxes

Income Taxes

File your own. The prices these CPAs charge is astronomical. The kicker is that they use the same software you can use on your own. Depending on how many schedules you must file based on your situation, the price varies on how much you can actually save. A small business owner could save two to three thousand filing their own state and federal taxes. *Cha-ching!* TaxAct is a great tool. It took some time for me to explore this option. A couple years ago I decided to file my own taxes. I started with the smaller company, and the overall cost was $60.00 saving me nearly nine-hundred. Now if that's not enough incentive, I don't know what is.

Property Taxes

Did you know that once you turn sixty-five you get a huge tax deduction on your property taxes? Well, you do. For those of you who have a long road toward senior citizenship, you have to aggressively appeal should you feel you're being overcharged.

Tax Deductions

Don't leave money on the table. Early on, I had a home office, and my accountant wouldn't allow me to take the deduction. "The IRS frowns on such things," he would say. I had a three-bedroom home, and one of those rooms was a fully equipped office running a viable publishing house. Copiers, printers, computer, laptop, the Internet, telephone, fax machine—all were inconsequential I was told. My two-car garage was dedicated to storing books. I never took the deduction. Get your deductions and save yourself money!

Insurance

Car

Keeping a clean driving history without infractions helps, coupled with an A-1 credit score. But with any insurance you have to be proactive. First, shop around for the best deal from a reputable company. The next thing to do to maximize savings is take the defensive driving course. They're offered online, and the average cost is $25.00. The course takes approximately six hours. However, upon completion, you get mandatory 10% reduction in rate for three years (depending on your state). Some states even offer a reduction in points. Do your research for your state and review your policy to make sure you aren't overinsured.

Homeowner's Insurance

There are usually three competitors, which vary per state. In New York, it's Allstate, State Farm, and Liberty Mutual. Get multiple quotes to determine the best deal. Should you pick a company and find that each year your quote increases and you have no claims on your account, switch. And remember, don't overinsure. It's wasteful. The insurance company won't pay out an inflated price, and the insurance agent gets a large commission on the policy. Natural disasters may not be covered under your policy. Flood and earthquake policies are usually separate. To avoid costly surprises, do your due diligence. Keep a log of all personal items, should you need to report a claim. You can do this by taking pictures and keeping a spreadsheet with the items and their costs. Or the websites and apps below could assist you:

◊ Encircle (free app)
◊ Belongings (free app)

Business Insurance

Be extremely diligent when choosing your business policy. Due to liability, you want to make sure you're fully covered for things like trips and falls.

Flood Insurance

If you are a homeowner, this is a situation where it is better to be safe than sorry. Most people have no flood insurance policy because their area is a low-risk of floods. With flood insurance, you must prepare for future risks. Natural disasters are getting worse and subsequently more frequent. The past is no longer a reliable barometer. Having an active flood insurance policy could end up saving you money. Trust me, I was one of the many Hurricane Sandy victims.

Food

Johns Hopkins Center for a Livable Future did a 2015 study which says each year up to 40 percent of our food goes to waste.

Shelf Life

Pay attention to the expiration date BEFORE you drop an item in your cart. Grocery stores stock dairy, meat and produce by placing newer items in the back. The items that are nearing expiration are pulled to the front. Pull bread from the lowest shelf for freshness. Once you get your food home, monitoring expiration dates is imperative. If you're like most of us and don't have the new refrigerators with Smart Fridge technology, then the apps below can assist with monitoring expiration dates[1] to avoid food spoilage, and also help you plan meals.

◊ Fridgely
◊ Foodfully

---

1   Sell by date: the date on perishables by which the food must be sold.
Best by date: the date which you should eat food for optimal taste.
Use by date: Is the last date recommended for freshest taste of food.

Multi-Meal Planning

Make a plan to avoid waste. Before you shop for groceries plan out your weekly menu. Buy ingredients that can be used for multiple meals and freeze and prep them to boost the convenience factor.

Avoid Instant Gratification

Avoid highly processed fast food. Fast food often is highly caloric, and has little nutritional value. Dollar menus can be tempting, but eventually could lead to medical issues if turned into a habit. And medical issues are expensive!

Cultivate

Grow fruits, veggies, and herbs to help balance your budget. You can start small, and if space permits, expand. Homeowners can take full advantage of this, but apartment dwellers aren't excluded. Container gardens are practical in any area where natural lighting comes through: windows, fire escapes, balconies, and terraces.

Don't be Bougie

Store brands are an excellent savings source. When I was younger, store brands were less tasty. Nowadays, you can't taste the difference, and usually these items are 20-25% less expensive. If you hold allegiance to brands you grew up on, or are weary of sinking money into store brands only to find them tasteless, then start small. Try switching out items such as condiments. Spicy mustard is a good starting point.

You Better Shop Around

You might hold allegiance to certain brands, but do not do so with supermarkets. Do price comparisons to see which store sells it for less. If store A sells meats for less and store B sells specialty items such as gluten-free for less, maximize your savings by shopping at both markets.

◊ Cellfire is a digital coupon app.

◊ Favado app helps you comparison shop local markets to maximize savings.

◊ Ibotta is a rebate app that pays you to shop. Payout: $10.00.

◊ Checkout 51 is a rebate app that pays you to shop. Payout: $20.00.

◊ SnipSnap app allows you to turn physical coupons into digital ones.

Bigger Isn't Always Better

ALWAYS watch the unit price even if an item is on sale. A common trick used to not only get you to purchase more is offering deals on bulk purchases. For instance, 4 cans of 9 oz peaches are "on sale" for $5.00. These cans are usually $1.39, so you would save a total of $0.56. However, the 16 oz can that's not "on sale" is $2.09. At first blush, you grab the 4 cans for $5.00. But when you do the unit price math, the non sale item is the better financial choice.

Incredible Bulk

If you have a large family, stock up on non-perishable sale items like tissue, paper towels, and cleaning products. Any products that get used up quickly in your household should be bought in bulk, on sale, and with coupons for maximum savings.

Chill Out

If you have freezer space or a deep freezer, buy family-size meats in bulk, contingent upon price. Clean, store, and date with freezer bags. *I also season meats before I freeze. Check out *Cheap Girls Club: Recipes* for more details.

Use What You've Got

Do not shop for groceries until your refrigerator is nearly bare. A mentor of mine uses this tip to save money, guaranteeing she doesn't waste what she has.

Lunchin'

A pull on finances is eating out at work. Prepare meals from home for breakfast and lunch, and save a huge percentage per week.

Cuppa Joe Cool

I'm often fascinated by adults who don't drink coffee. But if you're like most of us, and need your caffeine fix, I urge you to make your own. I need two cups per morning, per day. That could be a pricey habit. Some coffee drinkers buy 5- to 6-dollar cups of joe. Well, I'm not paying that. With flavored syrup and creamers, cinnamon, nutmeg, cocoa, and gourmet coffee beans, you are Starbucks. I don't get the Starbucks craze. Spending five bucks on gourmet coffee is insane. I've drunk my fair share, and it's like, "Eh . . . okay." No bells and whistles for me. You're buying into a lifestyle, like Apple. These powerhouses are selling an experience versus a product. It's a brand name, and when you hold that cup, it says you're one of the cool kids. If it's truly the taste you love, you can buy a bag of it at the grocery store and brew it fresh at home.

Dollar Dreams

You can find gems at these stores at a fraction of the price. My favorite is Dollar Tree, where things are actually a dollar or less. These stores have quality items, from cleaning supplies, food, snacks, school supplies, party supplies, and so much more.

◊ Dollar Store
◊ Dollar Tree
◊ Family Dollar
◊ Dollar General

Dine In

Although it's easy to breeze through a fast food line or sit at your local Olive Garden for a quick meal, dining in is the best option when you're on the trajectory to saving money. Dropping $30-$50 per meal per person on dinner you could have prepared yourself isn't helping to fatten your pockets. You can have "date night" at home.

Recreation

Group 'pon the Savings

Groupon is an excellent source to find activities for the family at a discounted rate. The membership is free, and they offer a wide variety of experiences, from fun and leisure to family outings and restaurant deals.

Work to Play

Volunteer at local concerts or festivals for perks and free shows. Volunteers get free admission, and depending on the venue, other amenities and promotional items, such as T-shirts, hats, and meal vouchers are allotted.

Save Stacks in the Stacks

You may want to consider—or reconsider—your local library. The library is truly the be-all and end-all of free entertainment. Libraries offer a buffet of music, movies, books, e-Books, and audiobooks. Some libraries even have free training classes.

Gifts

It's never a bad idea to put a spending limit on gifts. First, decide who should receive a gift and for which occasions. Reducing the frequency could save you upwards of 75%. If on average you spend $100 on gifts, four times a year that's $400. Limiting your gift expenditures to once a year with a maximum budget of $100 quickly saves you $300—75% in savings. You could plan for birthdays or Christmas—whichever, but just one.

Pooling

Let Me Ride

Car sharing is a good money saver. Whether it's to and from work or dropping children to and from school, the gas savings do add up.

Power in Numbers

Service pooling is a collaborative effort. If you live in a sub-division with homes in close proximity, contact service providers for group discounts. Usually, up to 15% is offered to homeowners for services such as garbage or snow removal.

Assistance

IDA's

Individual Development Accounts (IDA) are savings accounts for low-income people who meet the federal poverty income level. A dollar or more is matched for each dollar saved. This program is used for home and business ownership, or school loans. Check it out.

◊ http://cfed.org/programs/idas/directory_search/

◊ idaassist@cfed.org

Down Payment Assistance

Most states have programs to help first-time homeowners with down payments or closing costs. To be eligible for most you must be a first-time buyer and meet a host of other requirements. Homebuyers can gain assistance for a 1 to 4-family home, condo, or co-op in the 5 boroughs of New York through NYC Housing Preservation and Development. Please see below. The grant is up to $25,000.

◊ http://www1.nyc.gov/site/hpd/owners/homeowner-downpayment-assistance.page

Check your state for similar offers. If you qualify, you could save a lot of money on your down payment and use the saved money for an emergency fund, retirement, or home improvements.

If you are not a first-time homebuyer and need assistance in getting a reasonable mortgage with a small deposit, here are some programs to look into:

◊ Fannie Mae or Freddie Mac

◊ FHA: Federal Housing Authority ensures the loan to the lender. With this loan, the home buyer typically receives low-interest rates at 3.5%, is only required to make a small down payment, and incurs lower closing costs. Credit scores are less stringent too. You could qualify for an FHA loan with less than perfect credit.

◊ VA: The US Department of Veterans Affairs

◊ NADL

◊ Hud.gov

Affordable Housing

Affordable Housing[2] programs are available in most states. In New York, HPD offers assistance to low-to-moderate income families. Buildings are newly renovated and newly constructed. Applications are done online, and it is a lottery based system. You must meet a certain criteria, so review the guidelines before applying. If selected, you can find yourself in coveted areas of the five-boroughs at a fraction of the fair market value. These programs save you a considerable amount of money on rent.

◊ http://www1.nyc.gov/site/hpd/renters/find-housing.page

Mitchell-Lama Connect

For rentals and co-op apartments. The same steps apply as above. Follow the guidelines and see which program works best for you and your family.

◊ https://a806-housingconnect.nyc.gov/nyclottery/lottery.html#ml-home

Reimbursement

Renters

Get your security deposit back. So many renters end up losing their security deposits by being lazy and avoiding due diligence. Make sure

---

2   Each state has its unique program. Check your state for money-saving, affordable housing programs and save big.

you take pictures before and after you move in. Schedule and keep your walk-through appointment with your landlord and use your reliable smartphone to video the transactions. Just leave the property broom swept clean. That's it.

Unclaimed Funds

Years ago I closed out an account. I thought I was given all my cash. Approximately five or six years later I received a letter stating I had nearly two hundred dollars of unclaimed funds held by the state. It felt good. That was my earned money, and it was returned to its rightful owner. Here are some sites you can use to see if you have some "benjamins" with your name on them:

◊ https://www.usa.gov/unclaimed-money
◊ https://www.unclaimed.org/

Take That Back

I used to be the laziest shopper ever. I had energy for days to make the purchase, but if I got it home and it did not correctly fit or did not look as good as I thought, I would never take the time to do the return. The item would sit in the back of my closet or the trunk of my car until it was forgotten. Receipts would get filed away, and eventually I would move on. Now, before I make a purchase I always ask the store's return policy and make sure it's written on the receipt. I use a 3-day rule. I have three days to take back the merchandise. I've saved a ton of money just returning unused goods.

Don't Count on Them

Count your change when receiving it from all cashiers. They have a trick where they call out what they're supposed to give you, let's say, $3.78. You'll hear, "Three dollars, seventy-eight cents is your change." But what they'll place in your hands with the receipt is something much less. At the end of the night when they close out their register, they pocket the overage and walk away with your hard-earned money. Counting your change for accuracy takes seconds, and you'll be surprised how often a cashier has accidentally (or purposely) miscounted. Another thing to do is calculate your gratuity of your bill. Whether it's 15%, 18%, or 20%, add it up because an 18% tip could actually be 25% that you've just paid.

Food Tab

Always check your bill. While it could all be very innocent, if you look closely, you'll see you didn't order three salads or two baked potatoes. It's usually the smaller items added to your bill that often go unnoticed. If three people at the table order sides, a fourth side could be added, and if you don't check for accuracy, you could be paying for food you never ate. A famous New York restaurant with locations in ritzy areas such as New York, Beverly Hills, and London was allegedly investigated for overcharging their customers for years.

Laundry

Linens

Another trick to save you money is buying all-white linens and towels. This saves you money on laundry because you don't have to separate your loads from multiple colored sheets and towels. The bonus is it saves you time and effort.

Detergent

Use less of it for cleaner clothes. I remember when I would go to public laundromats I didn't feel my clothes were clean unless that front loading machine was bursting with sudsy bubbles. The truth of it is that we should not use the directions on the label and spot-treat each stain. More detergent won't remove the stain; pretreatment helps do that.

My front loading washer broke down and needed repair. I thought it would need a new motor. The technician came out and told me that nothing was wrong with the equipment. I had been using too much detergent. He ran the machine on "sanitize," cleared out all the built-up soap, and I've never had that problem again.

I wondered how I could use too much detergent when I followed directions. Then I reread the label, and it said this: "For medium loads, fill the cup up to the halfway mark. For larger loads use more." Use more? That's it. That's where I was taking my cue. Nowadays, I use no more than ¼ cup, and that's my max for large loads. I do an extra rinse, and I also cut out using fabric softeners. The smell lasts a few minutes and then it's gone, unless packed away in a sealed container. Fabric softener is also a waste on your finances. Using less detergent and no fabric softener will save you money!

Your Credit

A high credit score is beneficial. Lenders look at your rating and determine whether they will loan you money and at what cost. Good credit, for example, could net you zero interest on a typical 60-month loan. This could ultimately save you upwards of $4500 on a $40,000 fixed interest rate of 4.35%. A good example of how good credit will save you money is with a car loan. Dealers offer 0% APR if you have a score that falls between certain guidelines, netting you thousands of dollars in savings.

Animal Lovers

Stop going to these puppy mills where they breed animals for profit. Male dogs are studded out and females used as breathing baby factories. A veterinarian told me that some female animals have had so many births that their health is forever affected. Animal shelters have always been great staples in our communities. You can find pure and mixed breeds at a fraction of the cost of a breeder or pet shop. These animals are spayed or neutered, rabies vaccinated, and are up to date on shots, flea and tick repellent, and are microchipped. The nominal fee you'll pay is worth it. The low cost, usually $50-$100, pays for itself. And these animals are forever grateful.

Staycation

Vacations are great, and I love traveling. But a staycation could be just as awesome, if not better, because of the savings. A family of four could save thousands. Be creative, and remember to treat the home as if you're away from it. There should be no menial tasks—grocery shopping, laundry, cooking, and deep cleaning. Most importantly, don't work through your staycation. Office work and emails are off limits. Here are some neat ideas:

Glamping

If you have a tent, great, but you could find an inexpensive one at Walmart for under $30. You and your hubby or your whole family could sleep out under the stars if you have a backyard. If not, a deck, terrace, or your living room floor is fun too! Remember to take it seriously and add lanterns or white noise to contribute to the ambiance.

Movie night

If you don't own a projector, you could rent one for a relatively low rental price. Either in or outdoors this is a cool idea. Add the popcorn and candy and relax.

Picnic

Again, this can be done in or outdoors. If you prefer to stay in, have a carpet picnic with your loved one(s).

Hiking

It's free, and it's fun!

Sightseeing

Natives of any city rarely have time to do it. Walk around and see the city sights. Lazily stroll through parks and soak up the sun.

Game night

Always fun! Toss in cocktails and cold beers, and you have a recipe for ultimate escapism. Turn off those cell phones and get into vacation mode.

Travel

Hostel Takeover

Hostels are found in most countries on most continents. They are low-cost lodging, and Millennials love them. You save because the rooms and bathrooms are shared and often unisex. You won't have the privacy of a traditional hotel or motel, but the point is mingling with strangers from different backgrounds.

Stop and Save

An airport layover, when you have connecting flights to get to a final destination can save you money. If you have time to spare and want to vacation somewhere the tickets are usually steep, like abroad, then connecting versus nonstop flights are a good option.

Share the Love

Double to quad occupancy will save you tons when vacationing. The more people, the less expensive the trip. If you want to go to Paris, or Rome, or some exotic hot spot, think about getting friends interested. Splitting costs is always a wise decision. Couple that with a connecting flight, and you could save 25-40% overall.

Curve the Crowds

Traveling off-season could garner substantial discounts. Hotels and flights are usually less expensive, and you are not rubbing elbows with a lot of tourists. The biggest upside is the savings. You could get a five-star hotel at a three-star price. The downsides are that the hotels are not at full capacity so they can be understaffed and also the weather. If you are traveling to the Caribbean, then hurricane season is always a concern. If you're going abroad then cold and rain could put a damper on your trip.

Cruising

I love traveling by land and by sea. A cruise is a great option that could be inexpensive and save you money. As long as you're booking a reasonable cabin and not a suite (which many people don't know is even offered), then this is ideal for a couple, family, and retirees. The meals are factored into the price, but you do pay additional for certain amenities and upgrades. Each cruise line offers additional discounts to their loyal customers that are compounded with any promotions they are running. Single travelers benefit the least from cruises. You have to pay double occupancy. However, some ships offer a solo traveler discount—it's a small incentive.

◊ Royalcaribbean.com

◊ NCL.com

◊ Celebritycruiselines.com

◊ Carnivalcruise.com

Health

Everything in Moderation

Nothing matters—saving more, spending less, or investing for retirement—if you're not healthy. Paying attention to what you put into your body (reading food labels, staying away from over processed foods, GMOs, artificial colors, and flavors) coupled with exercise, could save you money in health bills.

The new mantra is, you can eat anything in moderation. I think everyone should be mindful of what we're serving on our plates and seek nutritional advice from our primary care doctors. No two bodies are alike, and what one body can easily break down and absorb, another may not. Between farm raised and wild caught seafood, whole versus processed foods, the tradeoff could literally manifest into adding or subtracting years of your life.

Warranties

Is the Juice Worth the Squeeze?

A good warranty can save you money. The million dollar question is whether your warranty is worth the paper it's written on. You can read the fine print, ask all pertinent questions, but the truth is that you won't know until something goes wrong with the product.

My relationship with warranties is on-again, off again. There has been a block of years I purchased them and years I did not. There is a two-prong approach to warranties. You can save money by not making the buy, or you can spend money to eventually save it, should the appliance need repair. Also note that warranty on parts, parts and labor, limited lifetime, and lifetime have vastly different meanings. If you want the added protection, then get it. But know what you're buying and if it's held by the manufacturer, the store where you made the purchase, or a 3rd party vendor.

Floor Models/ Overstock

In Plain Sight

From appliances to furniture, purchasing a floor model item saves you a ton of money. Speaking firsthand, I saved 70% on a floor model refrigerator, and when the delivery truck came with the wrong item, the store gave me an additional $250 gift card for my troubles. A floor model item might have a nick, dent, scratch, rip, tear, or some other deformity, but that's not the rule. Some items are in perfect condition. These gems are often overlooked because most consumers want things fresh out the box!

Too Much of a Good Thing

Overstocked items save you money too. Browse through your local home improvement stores which usually have overstocked items such as flooring, tile, or special order items such as window treatments.

Timing is Everything

Shop for the Best Deals During These Months

For aggressive discounts, I always recommend thrift shopping for secondhand first, and then Marshalls, Ross, Saks OFF 5TH, Last Call, HomeGoods, T.J.Maxx, and Nordstrom Rack. But sometimes you can't find what you want at discount retail chains and have to go the traditional route. Whatever you do, wherever you buy, always comparison shop, shop sale days, and use coupons if offered.

January

Winter Clothing/Outerwear: Toward the end of January and until inventory runs out through February, you can snag great deals on winter clothing and coats. Sales usually start at 50% off. Some stores offer stackable coupons, and you could walk away with a very good deal.

Fitness Equipment: January is the month for new resolutions, and fitness equipment goes hand in hand with the custom. Retailers usually offer up to 50% off fitness equipment to help us get started on our wellness track.

Christmas Ornaments: Seasonal décor is at rock bottom prices beginning December 26th through January. You can get up to 80% off on quality Christmas decorations for your home or business.

White Sale: This sale is held annually and has been going on for over a century. Consumers could expect to receive up to 50% discount on bed linens, towels, bedding, and household items. And you don't have to buy white to get the discount. Fine china can be purchased for steep discounts during White Sales.

Gym Memberships: As I said before, I am not a fan of gym memberships. Not because I don't believe in fitness and self-care, but because these memberships could be a drain on finances. However, January offers the best deals. Look for no money down, no contracts type of clubs with low monthly rates.

Flooring/Carpeting: Retailers know that homeowners usually want to upgrade their flooring before Thanksgiving and Christmas, and also during the summer months. So, in January, many retailers offer no-interest financing for 24 months and free installation, as well as lowered pricing and discount promotions on materials.

February

Mattresses: February has always been my month to save big on mattresses. There is no better feeling than waking up refreshed from a good night's sleep, and a good bed can assist with that. Look to save up to 50% on name-brand mattresses, and with some retailers, you can save more with stackable coupons.

Winter Clothing/Outerwear: Just as in January, the winter sales on clothing are phenomenal. There won't be a large selection left, but you can find great deals.

Tax Software: Goes on sale up to 50%, so procrastinators are winners here!

Theatre: In February theatres offer Broadway shows at a discounted rate when attendance is low. Also, you can get an even steeper discount by buying SRO tickets (Standing Room Only).

March

Chocolate: So Valentine's Day is done, and retailers still have stock left. Expensive chocolates such as Godiva and Ghirardelli offer steep discounts.

Frozen Foods: March has been deemed National Frozen Food month. Most likely you will see buy-one-get-one-free deals at your local supermarket. Clip coupons in February for stackable deals and extra savings.

Winter Clothing/Outerwear: In March, you'll find the last remnants of the winter season on sale. You can find great deals and stock up on clothing for you, your child, or as gifts.

Fitness Equipment: The fanfare of resolutions is over, so retailers use March to keep revenue coming in just as your resolve has started to wane. Fitness equipment is even lower in this month than in January.

April

Thrift Store Shopping, Clothes, Furniture, And Appliances: By tax season individuals are rummaging through their homes to get the tax deduction. Thrift stores are usually busting at the seams with donations. The rock-bottom prices won't necessarily be lowered more, but you should find a larger, better selection.

Travel: Booking for summer flights usually drops mid-April.

Vacations: Look for last-minute deals on cruises, European trips, and the Caribbean. In April, tourist crowds are thin; April is in the middle of winter holiday and summer travel. Hotel and flight deals are offered to keep revenue flowing through this lull.

Spring Clothing: If you still purchase your clothing from retailers, spring clothing will drop prices in April. Spring lines have been in stores for the two-month mark in April, so prices are cut to make room for summer items.

Home Improvement: As soon as the weather breaks, consumers get antsy and want to start home improvements. Big-box retailers know this, so they offer sales incentives to individuals wanting to buy materials to get a jump start on summer projects..

Tax Day Freebies: Look out for restaurants and coffee shops that offer freebies on April 15th.

Snow Equipment: Well, it's kinda hard to sell snow equipment when it's beach weather. Retailers provide steep discounts to clear out snow equipment.

Jewelry: Between Valentine's Day and Mother's Day, retailers offer discounts on jewelry to keep the cash flowing and avoid the lull.

Cookware: April offers good deals on cookware. Top brands go on discount during this month. If you're looking for new pots/pans, consider holding off until April.

May

Spring Clothing: Spring clothing go at a steep discount to make way for the summer collections. You can get upwards of 50% off, and with stackable coupons, you could save much more.

Home Improvement: Home improvement stores offer sales extended around this time and overlap into June.

Appliances: High-end appliances usually go on sale for up to 40% off.

Mattresses: May is a good month to save on mattresses, but I've found that February offers steeper savings.

Swimsuits: Swimsuits go on sale, but July and early August offer steeper discounts.

June

Lingerie/Swimwear: Victoria's Secret has placed lingerie on the map for June sales. Their semi-annual sale is legendary for the sexy minx in you. Swimsuits are also discounted this month.

Gym Membership: You can still find membership deals as late as June. Again, no commitments.

Tools: For Father's Day, tools are always at steep discounts. The irony is that most fathers do not want a machine or device as a gift on their special day, but that's what offered.

July

Clothing/Swimwear: Stores are already clearing out their summer inventory. Swimwear is discounted up to 50% and will continue to drop through August until supplies last.

Paint Sales: Lowe's and Home Depot usually discount house paint in July. The summer months are a good time to make home improvements.

Camping Equipment: Prices drop midway through the summer season. You'll get a discount and still have enough time to use your new finds.

August

Summer Apparel: You will get great deals on summer clothing in August; better than July. Most items will be on the clearance rack. You will most likely have to search for a good deal, but it's there.

Patio Furniture: You can easily find a large selection of discounted patio furniture, up to 50% off, right in time for your Labor Day weekend celebration.

Back To School Supplies: Office supply stores discount back-to-school supplies in August. Parents must comparison-shop and also use stackable coupons to save the most money.

Air Conditioners: If your old machine conked out mid-summer, or you're looking for a smaller, newer, or energy-efficient unit, air conditioners go on sale in August.

Travel: August through November has vacation deals as much as 50% off hotels, flights, and rentals. These months are relatively slow for establishments.

September

Grills/Lawnmowers: You can find good deals on grills and mowers in mid-September, after Labor Day, when you can save from 25-40%.

Summer Apparel: Whatever inventory is left, you can get exceptional deals on summer clothing, up to 80% off.

Patio Furniture/Cushions: Retailers must clean out inventory, so huge deals are offered. You can expect to find deals from 50-70% off.

New Vehicles: If you don't mind getting a current or prior year model, then you will find great deals on vehicles in September. Dealers offer stackable deals, discounts, or no interest for 60 or 72 months, or no-money-down type of deals.

Plants/Shrubs: Nurseries offer steep discounts on annuals and perennials to clean out inventory right before the frost. Stock up and plant perennials and watch them bloom next year for a fraction of the regular cost.

Appliances: Showrooms must get rid of older-model appliances. You can get great deals on older-model and floor-room-model appliances.

October

Jeans: High-end jeans usually go on sale in October, when you can find them at a fraction of the cost.

New Vehicles: Just as in September, the savings extend into October.

November

Televisions: Black Friday deals offer the best prices on larger-model televisions. The new 4K is an awesome buy during November.

Electronics/Laptops: Great Black Friday deals.

Wedding Dresses: If you have patience and a good eye, you can find your perfect wedding dress at up to 80% off. Designers are filling showrooms with their latest line, so you can get something wonderful without breaking the budget.

Contractors/Home Improvement: During the holidays and winter months when things tend to slow down, you can negotiate good deals for their services.

Home Winterization: Insulation, caulk, and tools to winterize your home can be found discounted.

December

Toys: Although you'll see sales on toys in November, you will get the best deals beginning the second week in December. By December 26th, those prices will drop drastically.

Christmas Decorations: Prepare for next year at rock bottom prices starting the day after Christmas.

Pools: If you have no pool and want one, then the winter is the time to get your deal. However, many homeowners are against adding a pool to their property, due to high maintenance costs, no return on their investment, insurance costs, and to avoid liability.

*Trick: How about literally freezing your credit cards? Dumping your cards in water and tossing them into your freezer could save you money! This is more of a delay than an all-out deterrent, but it could work as both. In theory, if you have to wait hours for your cards to

thaw before you can use them, you have time to think about it and to change your mind.

 ## Meditative Minutes

There are ways to save and best times to do so. However, the rule still remains: Just because an item was on sale, if you didn't need it, then you didn't save money, you spent it. Meditate for a moment in gratitude for what you have, not what you feel you lack.

 ## Cheap Girls Club Oath

I recently vowed to never make a full-price purchase on anything ever. When I go into my supermarket, I only buy the sales items, items for which I have a coupon, or two-for-one deals on items I need. I shop only for what's on my list, and I have stopped stocking up on things I don't need. Remember, full price is for suckers! Vow to not make one full price purchase for a full month. Even gas!

Chapter Four

Ways to Earn

We're all given a talent. Your job is to monetize it. Take a hobby and make it a brand name. If you can knit, how about designing hats, scarves or sweaters and selling them on the Internet, in local boutiques, or state fairs? Think I'm joking? Think again. There is a wife and mother of three who reportedly makes nearly a million dollars a year selling knitted headbands, scarves, and socks on Etsy. Motivated much? Well, she is.

Does billionaire Sara Blakely's story expand your views of what an idea can do for your bottom line? She created her Spanx brand, and as they say, the rest is history.

Mark Zuckerberg turned a social gathering site into Facebook and netted himself (and some shareholders) billions. He took an idea, paired it with his coding talent, and monetized it.

I ask, what's your talent? If you want to earn extra cash, then try to figure that out. Countless times I've heard people say they don't have talent, and that's just not true. Every person walking this earth was born with a talent, some more developed than others, but that's only because they honed it. The triple-threats of this world (a person who can act, dance, and sing) work hard to perfect their skills. But what about the rest of us? What can we do? Try jotting down five things that you love doing so much that you would do them for free. Ask yourself, what am I passionate about? You'll be surprised at what possibilities and potential you have. Doing

Jot down 5 things you love so much you'd do them for free.

something you love and making a living is everyone's dream. Start small with growth potential. Here are some ideas to get the money train rolling.

Daycare

Do you love children? Have enough room in your home or apartment? Why not consider opening an in-home daycare? Check your state requirements, but most states require that one adult person can look after five children under the age of ten. Good, flexible child care is hard to find for working parents. Are you a morning person? That could be a qualifier to get you hired. Some parents have an early commute and cannot find a daycare open during the wee hours of the morning. What about the evenings? Weekends? You could upsell your weekend services for couples who hold down employment on the weekends or work double shifts.

The average cost per child is $150 per week. A full house could gross you $750/week—that's a good source of income. Start small and then expand to a commercial location. Think bigger, Cheap Girls! What about expanding to a chain of locations? After you do your research according to your state, do not forget insurance. You will need adequate insurance to cover you against liabilities.

Blog

If you could be described with one word, would it be opinionated? Do you like having a voice, or being heard? Consider writing a blog. Blogs could be profitable, earning money through affiliations and advertisement sales. Pick an area that you're most interested in and go for it. Love spewing your thoughts on politics? Are you a conspiracy theorist? Love lifestyle, fashion? Are you a foodie? You could rake in upwards of six figures should your blog bring Internet traffic. You'll need to market and promote to get that traffic, but with hard work and dedication this could ultimately go from supplemental income to full-time employment.

Tutor

What I hear most from parents is that teachers have their plates full and don't have time to give their children the individual time they need to excel. These parents are two decades post-graduation, so trigonometry isn't rolling off their tongues. Brick-and-mortar tutoring businesses have inconvenient hours and are extra pricey. Being a genius in a particular subject doesn't necessarily mean you would be good at teaching it, so know your strengths and limitations. If you take this seriously, it could be a good way to earn.

Lessons

Hablas español, anyone? *Parlez-vous français?* If you're bilingual, I don't think it would be difficult promoting your services and landing clients. I would hire someone local to teach me French without hesitation. So think about it. It is a way to earn some money in your spare time. Listen, any specialized talent can be sold. It's the American way. Have you seen the Facebook pics from those paint parties? Wine and Design parties have been gaining momentum for some time now. To tell the truth, the end results don't look like a Picasso, but the hosts are selling an atmosphere. If you're a pianist, flutist, artist, bilingual, or trilingual, there is always a legal hustle out there. All you need is a little ingenuity and a lot of motivation.

Vacation Tour Guide

I've traveled to England, Ireland, Italy, France, Greece, Mexico, Cayman Islands, Turks and Caicos Islands, and the list goes on. But I didn't travel to those places in the #1 Cheap Girls Club way, which is free! Did you know that you could travel the world for free? You can earn free vacations if you do some research and put on your sales rep hat. You need no license to be a tour guide, but double check with your state. It would also be an excellent idea to write up an agreement to help protect everyone's interest. Also, have full disclosure. Let's say you pick England. You find, as an example, ten people to go for ten days. The costs for a nonstop flight, hotel, ground transportation, and tours around England tally to $30,000 for eleven people. The ten people that sign up for your England tour will each pay $3000, which allows you to have a fantastic free vacation. You are responsible for making sure the vacation goes off with no hiccups and that the accommodations equal what your vacationers have purchased. If everything goes well, you will have ten people that will re-book with you. There are many benefits of traveling in groups: group rates, safety in numbers, and peers to converse with.

A few years back I invited a friend to join me on my Italian vacation. I had gone there previously and fell in love with the country. We flew direct from New York to Milan and then to Rome. I had chosen the hotels, picked all the tours, and had car service waiting to pick us up at the airport. My friend was amazed that I was able to plan such an experience.

The world has evolved in such ways we can do, learn, or be most anything via Google. If I had the time, I would be a tour guide and get freebie vacations, as I love to travel. But since I can't, let me share this with my club.

Travel Deals

◊ Expedia.com

◊ Travelocity.com

◊ Priceline.com

◊ Cheaphotels.com

◊ Orbitz.com

◊ Trafalgar.com

◊ Trivago.com

◊ AAA.com

Excursions

◊ Viator.com

◊ Lonelyplanet.com

◊ Citysightseeing.com

Transportation

◊ Groundlink.com

◊ Supershuttle.com

◊ Airportshuttles.com

Housekeeping

Are you a neat freak? Can't walk past a messy bed or dirty dish without cleaning it? Need some extra cash and can't find employment? I bet you never thought you could find a job being someone's housekeeper. Well, you could. Some couples are even looking for live-ins (au pair) to keep their homes clean and orderly. Couples, bachelors, and single females are all looking for additional help, someone to come in and streamline their lives. Housekeeping could easily turn into a profitable business. Find a partner or hire independent contractors, but this field is certainly a consideration. Housekeeping services on average charge $85/hour but could go as high as $200/hour. Usually two workers are deployed, and a three-bedroom home usually takes two hours. Merry Maids started from an idea. Now they have national and international franchise locations.

Dog Walker

There is a real need in this occupation. Dog owners consider their four-legged friends a member of their family, and these "sons" and "daughters" have needs. They should be stimulated during the day while their owners are at work, fed, and shown affection. My neighbor has hired a dog walker for Lenny, a cute little Shih Tzu, who gets his daily exercise while his "mommy" is at work. Skeptics will think there isn't any money in this profession, but they're wrong. In the right location this service has real value. A highly populated city such as Manhattan, Chicago, or Los Angeles could net a self-employed person a reasonable salary. On a larger scale it could become a satisfying career. A catchy company name, reliable dog-walkers, and steady clientele are the key ingredients to having a viable business.

◊ **Fetch!** Is a pet-sitting franchise that could help you get your company up and running.

◊ **Snaggle Foot** also has franchise opportunities.

Product Endorser:

You love da 'gram? Check and post on Facebook ten times a day? Got many followers? You could think about contacting small companies and charge a fee to promote and endorse their product. Look for startup companies and small-product-based businesses. E-mail the company with your pitch outlining your social media accounts and followers. Agree on how often you could post a picture, link, or tweet about this product and at what cost. As with any business transaction, get everything in writing.

Virtual Assistant

This term is dated, but it's still a money-maker. If you've got mad organizational skills, then you can earn extra money as an assistant, since independent contractors, small businesses, and sole proprietors always need help.

The key to success in these suggestions is professionalism and trust. Handle yourself with the utmost respect, don't be combative, as the customer is always right. Most of all, have patience.

Personal Chef

Does everyone gather around at your home salivating for your next meal? Do you love mixing ingredients and trying new dishes, or sticking with the traditional dishes? It's all good, as long as it tastes good. There are more people who love to eat than cook. Look around you. Companies have popped up like toast in the past few years offering this very service. Think Plated, Blue Apron, and Hello Fresh. You could start off small, selling individual plates in your neighborhood. If you're good, then trust me, your services will spread by word of mouth. Being a personal chef isn't new. Years ago, I knew women who would sell plates of food to pay their rent, a common practice in lower-income neighborhoods. On the weekends they would flame up those burners and sell 3-4 course meals for $5 per plate. You could parlay your passion from your kitchen to a food truck. More recently, I read an article about two friends whose meals got so popular that residents near and far would drive to their home to purchase a meal. They made enough capital to open their own restaurant. Start small and watch it grow.

Hustle:

Consignment shops are a good way to earn some extra cash for specific wants, unexpected bills, or to make money while de-cluttering your home. You can bring your items to a physical shop in your area, like Plato's Closet. However there are many fabulous online consignment shops that expand the possibilities, regardless of your location.

◊ Poshmark
◊ TheRealReal
◊ Rebagg
◊ Thredup

If you live in a beachfront, urban, or ski community, you can rent out your bike, surf, and snowboard sports equipment for extra cash. Sharing resources helps reduce your carbon footprint.

◊ Spinlister.com

Meditative Minutes

Take a few minutes to meditate on your passions, your likes, your dreams, and open your mind to possibilities. Let the positive energy flow!

Cheap Girls Club Oath

You must be a driven and creatively thinking female to think of ways to earn additional income. Don't put pride before the grind, or you will stay broke. When you put your mind to finding supplemental income, you can't give up. At first glance, it seems easy. It's not. It's simple enough to start, but the challenge will come trying to sustain it. This Club is for winners—women with goals, vision, and who are ready to roll up their sleeves and work hard. If you're not willing, you can exit on Broke St.

Chapter Five

Unpretzel Your Debt

*Y*ou've decided that you want financial freedom. You long for the life you've imagined for you and your family. The thing is, procrastination trumps good intentions. Next week turns into six months, and before you know it, a year has passed. With interest. Your debt has grown, and you're no closer to getting a handle on your finances. You sit back down and wonder what happened. How do you level up to the Cheap Girls Club penthouse? Where do you start? The ground floor, of course.

Types of Debt

Credit

◊ Credit Cards
◊ Store Cards
◊ LOC – Line of Credit for Businesses
◊ HELOC – Home Equity Line of Credit

Loans

◊ School Loan
◊ Auto Loan

◊ Business Loan

◊ Home Improvement Loan

Mortgage

◊ Personal Mortgage

◊ Real Estate Investment

Medical

◊ Healthcare Insurance

◊ Medical Bills

Taxes

◊ State Income Taxes

◊ Federal Income Taxes

◊ Property Taxes

Definitions

◊ Variable Interest Rate – The APR3 varies until the loan is paid off.

◊ Fixed Interest Rate – You maintain a fixed rate for the entire loan.

◊ Revolving – Available up to a certain limit and can be continually used on a reoccurring basis.

◊ Unsecured Debt – No collateral.

◊ Secured Debt – Collateral.

◊ Income – Money earned from work, investments, interest, business, or alimony, child support, structured settlement, or annuity.

◊ Asset – Property owned by a person or company that has value and does not carry debt.

◊ Versus:

◊ Liability – Something (such as the payment of money) for which an individual or business is legally responsible.

---

3   APR is the annual percentage rate lenders charge.

To unpretzel our debt, we must break it down and get real about certain misconceptions. It's OK to play along, but don't play dumb. When I purchased my first home, I had a mortgage. That was the first and last time I used a mortgage to buy real estate. I did not convince myself this was "good" debt; it was, purely, debt. Good debt is a misnomer. When I sat down with the mortgage lender and he went over my down payment, credit score, interest rate, and how this was a "good" deal, I smiled, nodded, and played along. But he wasn't ever going to convince me that debt was good. We all should know going in that good debt is a fallacy—a rationalization from lenders to get us to take out loans.

Sure, you can get a good mortgage loan with a low fixed rate to purchase rental properties. And those resources could place income into your account each month. Well, great. You've made an institution work for you. But what if you never found a renter? I had one rental sit on the market for eleven months without a tenant. It happens. It had to be heated in the winter, security system active, utilities paid for outside security lighting, cooled down during the hot summer months, property taxes, insurance—the whole umbrella of ownership. Now, what if I also had a mortgage to add to those expenses? The phantom of good quickly turns on you.

Yes, you can get a school loan to pay for an awesome education. But how about all those who can't find gainful employment in their field and default on those student loans? Not so good, eh?

Personally, I feel that a major contributor of Americans getting into debt is that we were taught to differentiate between good and bad debt, when, truthfully, no debt is good.

Here's what we were brainwashed into believing:

The Illusion of Good Debt

◊ School loan

◊ Mortgage

◊ Business start up loan/Business investment loan

◊ Investment property/real estate loan

Believed to Be Bad Debt

◊ Automobile loan

◊ Credit cards

Debt listed as sound can be a necessity to some, even most, but the term "good debt" has given us a false sense of financial acuity, allowing us to choose between the lesser of evils. If managed correctly, credit/loan debt can help you attain wealth should you purchase, let's say, a home that ultimately increases in value. You sell it, make a profit, and everyone is pleased. But a more conventional reality can happen, and you learn that property doesn't always appreciate in value. Your mortgage is under water, and you have negative equity in the property you thought was a wise, profitable investment because the masses had it listed in the "good" debt column. I was brainwashed too. But post-2008, a mortgage in the "good" column became the exception and not the rule. Debt should not have been broken down and simplified enough to merit a "good" label in first place. Labeling something as "good debt" should be conclusory—only after a profit has been made, not before.

So here we are, with good debt staring us in the face, and she doesn't look cute. She looks just as ugly as bad debt. When the monthly bills hit, I promise you the school and auto loans all feel the same when you're scrimping to make ends meet.

Now let's get to work. It's time for a reality check. Gather all your current debt statements, good or bad, fixed or variable—anything you owe money on, even if you consider it an asset—and plug the balances due into a spreadsheet. Google Docs has a host of free financial spreadsheets that are user-friendly. Once you do this, decide how YOU want to pay them off and place those items in chronological groups. Here's why. Different people have different expectations and core beliefs on how they see debt. Some people don't see a mortgage as a liability, so they're in no rush to pay it off. The 30-year loan works best for them. I agree that you shouldn't introduce an added pressure of paying off your mortgage if you feel strongly about monthly payments and also if you don't have a practical way to pay it off. And remember the school loan is listed in the Good Debt column, yet we should definitely want to rush to pay that off. School debt (along with tax debt) is the only debt you can't forgo when filing bankruptcy. So this debt shouldn't be ignored.

When I was unpretzeling my debt and creating a budget, I wanted it all to go. But that might not be realistic for everyone. Paying off debt comes after you've created a budget, are current on all your bills, cut costs, and found surplus or supplemental income. Your supplemental income could come in the form of cutting or lowering costs, a raise in salary, or a second job.

 Paying off debt comes after you've created a budget, are current on all your bills, cut costs, and found surplus or supplemental income.

Activity Time!

The spreadsheet should look like something this:

Cumulative totals	$313,500
Credit Card	$5,000
Student Loan	$35,000
Medical Bills	$2,500
Taxes	$4,000
Auto Loan	$17,000
Mortgage	$250,000

Five-Year Payoff Benchmark:

◊ Credit cards

◊ Medical bills

◊ Car loan

◊ Uncle Sam

Seven-Year Payoff Benchmark:

◊ Student loan

Fifteen-Year Payoff Benchmark:

◊ Mortgage (optional)

Get the gist? Great, but how do we choose a benchmark? Once I had pulled my outstanding payables into a spreadsheet, cut costs, and lowered my overhead, I was able to see how much extra cash I would have each month. Doing the necessary cuts would allow me to see a savings of $10,500 in additional business monies each month. Next, I used a payoff calculator which outlined that I could be debt-free within 24 months.

Now here are two highly successful methods to help you implement your Payback Plan.

Avalanche Method

You allocate any extra money to the debt with the highest interest rate first while paying the minimum on all other debt. This method allows you to save the most money, but some argue that tackling the largest debt first could feel overwhelming and the likelihood of continuing on your path to financial freedom could be hampered, if not deterred indefinitely.

Debt Snowball Method:

Made well-known by Dave Ramsey (love him), this approach is the complete opposite of the avalanche because you pay off the smallest debt first and continue paying the minimum on all other debt. Once that little debt is paid, you move on to the next one, until you ultimately reach the largest debt. The theory here is that getting rid of debt one bill at a time keeps you motivated and you are more likely to see success.

One approach saves you money, the other keeps you motivated because you see victory early and often. These are personal choices. For me, it made sense to tackle the largest debt with the highest interest rate because ultimately it would save the most money. I owed so much money that every penny counted. I was fed up, I was focused, and I did not need extra motivation to get the debt paid off, so I began with the highest interest rate and worked my way down. I had to fight my way back to zero, and that's exactly what I did. Below, I am listing a snapshot of what my largest debt looked like. Although it was business debt, I was the guarantor on the loans.

Avalanche Example

Debt	Principal	APR	Renewal Fee	Minimum Payment
Bank of America Business Line of Credit	$35,000	5.5	$0	$1050
Chase Business Line of Credit	$56,000	5.5	$150	$1680
Citibank N.A. Business Line of Credit	$200,000	9.78	$150	$6000

I added my debt into a payoff calculator (see below) with a payoff goal of 24 months. I found ways to save, cut operating costs, and I managed to come up with an additional $10,500 monthly to go toward debt repayment. Had I chosen the snowball method, I would have paid off the Bank of America LOC in less than four months, then moved on to Chase, and then tackled the largest debt with the highest APR, Citibank.

In 24 months, using the Debt Snowball method, I would have paid $22,701.69 in interest. Using the Avalanche method, I ended up paying out $16,369.56 in interest, with a savings of $6332.13. Every. Penny. Counts. For me! Get that ingrained in your mind down to the smallest form of currency, a penny. Most people walk past a penny when they see it lying on the floor, but see the value in it. Welcome to the club!

Snowball Example

Debt	Principal	APR	Minimum Payment
Mastercard	$1,500	13.99	$45
Visa	$1,800	13.99	$54
AMEX	$2,200	23.99	$63
Car Loan	$17,000	9.5	$515
Student Loan	$35,000	4.8	$1,000

You pull in some extra hours working the weekends and net an additional $550/month. You also cut costs, lowered your utilities, and got rid of your cable, which saves you $200/month. You now have an extra $750 per month to pay down debt. MasterCard will be the first bill to tackle while making minimum monthly payments on the others. It will take two months for MasterCard to be paid in full. With the now freed up money you take the now $795 ($750 + $45 minimum payment) and apply that toward paying down Visa. As you knock out your debt, the elimination of cards should help keep you motivated.

Payoff Calculators

◊ Nerdwallet.com
◊ Bankrate.com

Steps I Took to Unpretzel My Debt

1. Decided that my debt needed to be paid off.
2. Gathered my most recent statements and placed them into a spreadsheet.
3. Looked for savings, made budget cuts, and found supplemental income to toss at debt.
4. Created a budget using free financial software, which you'll find in Chapter Seven.
5. Found a free online payoff calculator.
6. Chose a debt payoff method (Avalanche worked for me; however the Debt Snowball has a high success rate).
7. Took action.

Free Debt Counselors

Should you find yourself in a situation where you feel you need professional help with your debt, breathe a sigh of relief that there are services available to give you guidance. Below are great resources to utilize for credit counseling, budget planning, and money management tips.

◊ National Foundation for Credit Counseling
◊ GreenPath
◊ Consumer Credit Counseling Services

Unpretzeling your debt should feel empowering. Once you put together your Payback Plan (budget plan + method), then you're winning. Pat yourself on the back because it takes a wise person to know that all hell has broken loose and you need to overcome debt. For whatever reason, you have found yourself owing either a person or an institution. But you have good sense to go back to the beginning to dissect the monstrosity we call debt. You don't have to accept being in debt. It's something you can fix. It's time to get thrifty. Be cheap. It's an invaluable core value. It's the "secret" no one wants to share.

What I feel that I have to stress is that you cannot pay down or pay off debt unless you find additional money. If your paycheck has just enough wiggle room to make minimum monthly payments

You can't pay off debt unless you find additional money.

on your current debt, then choosing a debt method is inconsequential. You can't apply the Debt Snowball or Avalanche methods without additional funding. You may have read things like, "Add an extra $200 toward this credit card each month, or that loan biweekly, and you should have that debt paid off within six months." But $200 from where? This is why the Ways to Save, Ways to Earn, and Make Debt an Asset (coming up next) chapters are imperative. Because none of this is possible without more money! And then, obviously, all else follows. *Capisce*?

 ## Meditative Minutes

Take a few moments to meditate on your strengths. Know that you're an overcomer and nothing that comes up against you shall win. Not even debt. You can beat this. Now all you have to do is believe it.

 ## Cheap Girls Club Oath

Make a vow that you will never, ever be on the wrong side of debt again. If debt feels like a calculus equation, remember it is not. If you look carefully, you will understand that debt is simple addition and subtraction. Take the oath to stop spending!

Chapter Six

Make Debt an Asset

For decades, we were taught that a home was an asset. Over the past 20 years, financial advisors sounded the alarm dispelling this myth. The logic is simple—If you owe, it's debt, and if you own, it's an asset. No wiggle room. This is an often controversial rule. Universally, homeowners wanted to assert that their home was an investment, and, therefore by default, an asset. In theory, that outlook seemed sound. Then the Great Recession of 2008 hit and things got topsy-turvy. Homeowners realized what the advisors had warned was true: Your home is debt, not an asset!

But what if we could tip the scales? It's the glass is half full/half empty outlook. Let's discuss whether your glass is half empty. Most people say they are homeowners when their bank owns the title of the home until it's paid off. The borrower owns the debt usually for a thirty-year or less timeframe, depending on how quickly they reconcile their account.

For this book, I had the privilege of interviewing numerous women for the Cheap Girls Club workshop within the age demographic of 18-50. The workshop, through my church, was a convenient way to allow people with similar shortcomings to have a sounding board.

For this chapter, two friends stood out in the small focus group I was conducting. There was a little rift brewing between two women who looked at debt differently. Both women were attractive, dressed trendily, and on the surface both seemed to be on solid financial ground.

Let's start with Kim. At thirty-five years old, she is a quiet, ambitious woman. She has been investing for retirement since she was twenty-seven, owns five properties, all liquid, and is a business owner. Of the five properties, one is her home, three are rentals, and the fifth is a commercial building where she rents space to small business owners. Kim is unmarried with no children. She receives income from her investment properties and also from the two pizza franchises she co-owns.

Then there's Victoria. Victoria is employed at a large-cap corporation, married, and has three children. She's forty-years old and recently bought her first home with her husband after previously being a tenant in one of Kim's rentals at a discounted "friend" rate. Victoria works a lot of overtime, usually doing doubles, to purchase the "wants" and maintain the "needs" of life.

These two women clashed because Victoria wanted Kim to see her as her financial equal, if not superior. I found this fascinating. Victoria felt

If you owe, it's debt. If you own, it's an asset.

that she had the home, the car, the kids, the mate, the job—that she was living the American dream. Kim's wasn't knocking what Victoria had, but it wasn't what Kim felt was ideal for her. The spat went like this:

"Well, you know what I think? I believe you got very jealous when I bought my home. When I told you that we were going to get our floors redone and we were going to pay fifty thousand, you didn't have anything to say."

Calmly, Kim replied, "Victoria, I did say something. I asked how you two were going to pay for those floors, and when you answered that you two would work overtime and pull from your 401K, well, there's not much to say after that."

Victoria desperately wanted to get a rise out of Kim. She screamed, "Exactly! You were jealous because my husband and I were getting so much overtime and my house was going to look beautiful, just as good as yours!"

Kim shook her head. "Vicky, you keep screaming that I'm jealous. I let it go because I didn't want to argue with your delusion. What I didn't want to say to you because I didn't want to seem as though I was big-headed is that I am not even somewhat jealous. I solely own five properties that I paid for in cash, four of which generate income to fully support my life. You have 50% ownership in debt for the next 30 years. You"—Kim did air quotes—"'own' half of one property. One, Vicky. It's so ridiculous that I never thought I had to justify your rant with a statement, but obviously, I do."

Victoria thought for a second about what Kim had said, but you could tell she didn't process it. "I don't care what anybody has to say. You were jealous!"

Kim shrugged. "If you say so."

"I do!"

"You know, I was happy when you got the house. But I've come to realize that you do not want me to be happy for you. You want me to be jealous of you."

"I don't care what you say. I know in my heart you're jealous that I bought a house and you don't want my floors done."

"I own. You owe."

As both women spoke, I wondered what this situation was really about. At its core, was it about flooring? These women embodied the juxtaposition of this argument: Is your home debt or an asset?

Victoria, like most, convinced herself that her home was a great investment. When she and her husband sat at that closing table, she felt she'd done something remarkable. If homeownership was the endgame, then she won. Just note that homeownership isn't for everyone, and "ownership" isn't ownership until you own it outright. If you should be in a financial position to go through the process to get a home loan, whether it's for

It isn't ownership unless you own it outright.

three hundred thousand or three million, you shouldn't feel superior to anyone, let alone someone operating on as full a tank as Kim was.

But what I found odd with Victoria is that she felt she and her husband adding $50K floors trumped owning outright. She was so committed to her flooring that her tunnel vision blocked the message Kim was trying to put forth. I find Victoria's position to be insane.

Is homeownership a need or a want? Did she chase a 30-year mortgage just to make it an Instagram-able moment? Was the dog and pony show all to conclude that her friend or friends were jealous of engineered wood floors? When you enter into the fortieth year of your life, shouldn't you be able to definitively conclude what is or is not an asset? No? Not yet. How about 50? When you turn 50, should you exhale because you've gotten your first home that won't be yours until you're 80? These are the questions one must ask oneself to avoid the limited views of Victoria.

Now let's delve into Kim's perspective. She was passionately investing wisely and generating income from her investments. Back in the '90s when the economy was thriving, millionaires liked to say they could live off their interest. With banks offering interest rates as low as .02%, and five-year CD rates less than 2%, the glory days of living off interest for the average earning person are over. Contrary to what Victoria thought, Kim was living her dream. She had financial freedom. She had zero debt. Did Kim have the infamous flooring in her homes that Victoria so famously stated she was jealous of? Absolutely. So how could Victoria even fathom this was a point of contention? Well, that's more a Dr. Phil problem than a money issue. For me, even though the logic is absurd, it is conventional wisdom.

But how does this help us? Everyday people with 30-year mortgages aren't in the same position as Kim. Yet, society has us thinking they are. The Kims of the world who purchase assets all liquid are not operating on the same level as the Victorias, but on the surface, people just can't seem to understand that. Why? Why are they seen as equals? All we see is the visual (the home). How many people peel back the layers to see what's really there (debt)?

Let's say you bought a home for $500,000. Your budget was $350,000, but the realtor kept showing you properties way outside your price point, and you bit. You put (as an example) $5000 down and you have a mortgage loan of $495,000 for 30 years. Your mortgage is $3800/month (including taxes and insurance), and after 30 years you've paid $1.3 million to the bank, nearly triple the original loan. Seems like debt to me. Even if in 30 years you sell the home for $1.4 million (there are so many variables that buying a home is like gambling), you think that you've just made a $905,000 profit. Even the seller's realtor will count $905,000 as earned profit. Your broker will ask you, when determining the list price, what you originally bought the property for. So you do the math, and you think that you've made the most, $905,000 in profit, less fees. Everyone is happy—let's celebrate. But then you do the math and realize you've paid the bank $1.3 million throughout the 30-year fixed loan, and the windfall isn't as celebratory. And then you subtract the cost to maintain the property—landscaping, renovations, upkeep, HVAC and roof replacement—and you walk away with a learned lesson. Homes are money traps. Now had you bought that home thirty years ago, all liquid, for $500,000 and sold it for $1.4 million, you can safely note that your asset was a significant investment. See the difference?

I remember I was in my late teens, and my best friend, Stephanie, was ten years my senior. Her boyfriend had purchased her a luxury car paid for in cash. A year later a friend of ours, Lisa, got a fancy SUV too. Both women had the keys to ideal vehicles for the entire world to see. However, I will never forget what Stephanie said to me. "I wish Lisa would stop going around saying her boyfriend bought her car. How can you own a car that still has a car note?"

I was clueless. My mind searched for understanding. I replied, "Well, he was the one who put the down payment on the car for her."

"And she has to pay her car note each month."

"Yeah, but she said it's low."

Stephanie rolled her eyes. She was upset that Lisa would even make the comparison and connect the situations and also that I couldn't decipher the difference. "Chris, she's giving him too much credit. If they wanted to say that he bought her car, then he should have *bought* it."

Honestly, I didn't get it. Didn't most of us have car notes? And did it matter if Lisa had a car note and Stephanie did not? What I saw were two women with pricey vehicles way above my pay grade. I was impressed with Lisa and Stephanie equally. What I didn't understand at that time was that Stephanie was on to something way back then. She knew that as long as someone can come and repossess your car, then you don't own it. If you're still confused about ownership, just ask that question: Who can take this away from me?

Now that we can all agree that your home and car are debt, how can we turn our debt into an asset? Well, I'm glad you asked. How about renting a room in your home? Renting rooms isn't for everyone, and like most life-changing decisions, it requires a lot of thought before taking the plunge. Renting rooms had a stigma before Airbnb, but now more people are taking it into consideration to help make the mortgage.

In my small group, I suggested that a woman rent out her bedrooms. Carol is a 43-year-old divorcée. She and her husband got married right out of high school and bought a huge Victorian in a college town. She had eight additional rooms and had spent years restoring the home to its glory. In the divorce settlement, her husband got the fifty acres of land they jointly owned, and she kept the house. She explained that they had put so much work into the home, she couldn't part with it. She was emotionally attached to it, whereas the husband thought financially and took the land. He sold forty acres and kept ten. With the remaining ten he leased a few acres and built himself a modest-size home. To Carol's dismay, it seems he got the better deal.

Carol's mortgage is $1700/month, but with essentials and nonessentials, her monthly bills are just slightly above $3000. I am not a financial advisor. I repeat that's not what I do. However, I am a good listener, and I have suggestions for my Cheap Girls Club. I asked Carol how comfortable would she feel as a single woman renting out rooms in her home, and she replied, "I should be fine."

Renting out rooms to subsidize your mortgage could be profitable. Depending on the area, rooms could rent for approximately $1200-$1500/month. Carol's area and home couldn't justify that much, but she hired a realtor[4] who did the background checks, collected the security deposits, and brought the potential renters to her. When we'd first discussed this option, we both assumed that college students would fill up most of her rooms. However, the rooms rented to divorcees— men and women, people on fixed incomes, and expats. Carol moved to her basement, which was nearly one thousand sq. ft. She rented out the upstairs master bedroom with en-suite bathroom for $900/month and six modest-size bedrooms for $550/each. Carol was now bringing in $4200/month, and she covered the utilities. The moment Carol got a gain and not a loss, her debt turned into an asset. She could cover her mortgage with the income she made from that property without having to work a nine-to-five. She could go away on vacation, climb Mount Rushmore, hike the Appalachian Mountains, and still generate income.

Should you not want to rent your rooms for long durations, you could consider listing your home on sites for vacationers, businesspeople who don't want to stay in a hotel, or family that travel out of state for events such as weddings. There is money out there, and enough for everyone, and we Cheap Girls want in! Why should hoteliers get all the capital when you have something equally good to offer?

When pricing your rooms consider these things

◊ How close is your home to transportation? Restaurants? Nightlife? Entertainment?

◊ Are you close to landmarks or tourist attractions?

◊ Decide what you're selling. Is it convenience? Is it a rural retreat with a private master bedroom, pool, and seclusion?

---

4 You do not need to hire a realtor. You can list your rooms yourself via social media, word of mouth, signage, or referrals.

Here are sites that could help you turn your debt into an asset.

◊ Airbnb.com

◊ Vrbo.com

◊ Flipkey.com

◊ Homeaway.com

◊ Tripping.com

Now, these suggestions won't be for everyone, but they could be a consideration. There are precautions, though. Should you decide to move forward with any of the above options, please get Host Protection Insurance if the rooms are rented for short durations. If you have long-term tenants, please contact your homeowner's insurance and get a policy according to your new situation. Renting a room is considered business activity, and generally, homeowner's insurance does not cover this. It is imperative that you are sufficiently covered. Adequate insurance will save you money against liability in the long run, should an unforeseen accident occur. And don't forget about Uncle Sam. This is taxable income which must be reported.

Don't want to rent to strange adults? OK, I hear you! Let's look at another option. How about opening your home to foster children? This might be controversial, but I have good intentions with this one. If you're maternal, have lots of love in your heart, and love children, it could be a consideration. There are so many children living in the foster care system who need good, loving, reliable homes. The state pays for the child's essentials with a monthly stipend, a portion of which goes toward rent. This isn't a "get-rich" hustle and shouldn't be considered a come-up. To qualify, you have to be employed or have an income (disability, alimony, palimony, social security), so if you're thinking about living on the child's state check, don't. These kids need love and guidance, so do not take this situation lightly.

Depending on your location, a car may be the only form of transportation. Public trains and buses may not run in your area. Most of us get a car for convenience. Generally, the purchase is either for vanity or practicality—a Benz vs. a Camry. Whatever the level of need for a vehicle, you have one. And each month it is getting harder to pay the note and/or car insurance. Here comes Uber, the cool-sounding, trendy startup, rappers-dropping-its-name-in-songs company. Notwithstanding the negative press—please always consider safety first—driving for a company such as Uber where you design your work schedule is smart. You could easily turn your car debt into an asset. Let's say you have a $300 car note. A friend of mine says he could make that in four days, working part-time in Brooklyn, New York.

Uber could be an option, and isn't an answer for everyone. Like anything else where risk is involved, make sure you do your research. Read their employment contract, and decide if this is something that could be a solution. Here are two companies you could look into should you want to consider being an independent contractor and use your personal vehicle:

◊ Uber

◊ Lyft

 Meditative Minutes

If it makes dollars, it makes sense. Before you sit with idle hands and allow your home to go into foreclosure, or the bank to repossess your car, be proactive and make debt an asset. Meditate first on the pros and cons. Allowing people into your personal space is life-altering in ways that can be beneficial, or not so much. See how you feel after some quiet sessions on the matter.

Cheap Girls Club Oath

Promise that now that you've committed to being in the Cheap Girls Club that you will thoroughly research all deals before taking on new debt. Once you're in, only money can get you out.

Chapter Seven

Budget? What's That?

*I*t's something you should get down with. It forecasts your monthly expenditures, likely income, and helps you monitor wasteful spending. A budget helps you make room for what's important to you. You want to save for your child's college fund? Your budget could help you find that additional $50 per month needed to sock away in a 529 Savings Plan. You want to retire at 50 years old? A budget could help make that possible. Yet few people have one. Look, even though our government can't seem to balance our national debt, I promise your finances are less complex, should you just take a look-see.

It doesn't matter how large or small the paycheck, not one person has unlimited funds. The richest person on earth can either spend or lose it all. Having a budget will allow you to prepare for emergencies, at least for the foreseeable future. A budget is non-negotiable.

The experts use a breakdown similar to these to help estimate your income and how you should be allocating it.

Zero Sum Budget

Is exactly how it sounds. Basically, zero-sum budgeting forces the allocation of every dollar you make to something. It's a comprehensive, detail-oriented tool that leaves no room for splurges or unnecessary spending. This budget has no leftover funds. Each dollar should be allocated toward rent, retirement, savings, investing, or debt repayment, as examples. Should you have ten bucks left over at the end of the month, well, you're not done budgeting. Your monthly CFO duties aren't complete until you tell that ten dollars where to go. This is the real deal. Every penny has a purpose. You take your salary, deduct your expenses, and have zero dollars left. This restrictive budget would be great for a spendthrift. But before you decide to marry this budgeting method, note that it uses your prior salary (January) to pay this month's (February) bills. So you'll need to have one month of income saved.

Some jobs don't have overtime, so your paycheck is the same each week or biweekly. When I worked for a particular law firm we didn't get overtime, so I had to find a second job to supplement my cash flow. If your salary is consistent, then creating this budget should be simple with free financial software (listed below).

Cash-Only or Envelope Budget

I began hearing about the cash-only budget through my church some years back, and Dave Ramsey's name was attached to it. His "envelope system" was what my grandmother and her ancestors had been doing for decades. This budget, I thought, was primarily known throughout lower-income neighborhoods. My grandma's system would take the cash from her paycheck and place all categories into envelopes: food, rent, utilities, et cetera. Each area of her life had an envelope, and if an unexpected bill came up, well, it would have to wait until the following pay period.

Dave Ramsey's system has been updated to include only those items that you don't pay for with a check or auto-debit. Not many people pay rent or utilities in cash. This system is standard, and I get why it works for most. However, this could never work for me because I know my shortcomings. Having envelopes stuffed with cash just lying around until I physically went to pay the bill would be like having candy in front of a baby. Too much temptation. My self-control would be nil, and I would dig myself deeper into debt.

Balanced Money Formula

This budgeting system, created by Elizabeth Warren, is what I used.

The 50/30/20 or 50/20/30 rule goes like this:

◊ Half of your net income should be allotted for your "needs," your essentials.
◊ Thirty percent can go toward "wants," nonessentials.
◊ The remaining twenty percent should go toward savings, debt repayment, and retirement.

But what about those of us who want to allocate more toward retirement? That 20% to be divvied up between savings and debt repayment seems paltry. For my retirement each year I max out the highest allowable percentage for contribution by the IRS, which is currently at 25%. So the 50/30/20 rule doesn't work for me in its original form. And that's OK. You can make your own rules up, just as long as the end result accounts for 100% of your income. Whether your rule is 50/20/20/10 or 50/25/15, it's all what works for your situation and goals.

I took a closer look at that 30% of "wants," the nonessentials, and made some serious cuts, and then reduced a couple things in my essentials, 50%. So my pie chart might've looked like this:

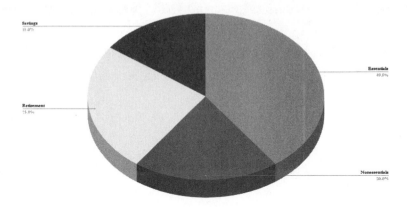

Take a look at what to list under needs/wants and have a go at shaping your own breakdown.

Essentials:

◊ Rent

◊ Mortgage

◊ Car note

◊ Insurance(s) – auto, homeowners, renters

◊ Utilities

◊ Credit card minimum payments

◊ Groceries and household necessities

◊ Healthcare

Nonessentials:

◊ Cell phone

◊ Cable and/or the Internet

◊ Entertainment/social life

◊ Beauty needs (toiletries, hair care, nails, other)

◊ Clothing splurges

Some bills have blurred lines and could fall between the two. Groceries should be on the essentials, since it's a need. However, snacks would fall under nonessentials. Clothing is another that could be nitpicked. Buying that little black dress when you already have ten makes it a nonessential. Anything that is not absolutely necessary to survive, any non-priority debt is basically a want. When you're looking for savings, look to the nonessentials first and then move on to essentials. You could find that money by moving to a lower-priced rental, or finding savings with where and how you shop for groceries. Refer back to the Ways to Save chapter for more ideas.

Pay attention to the tiniest minutia when analyzing your finances. Always remember, it's just as important to save money as it is to make it. You must police yourself into spending within the boundaries of your household budget and not loosen the reins until you're sitting on a

It's just as important to save money as it is to make it.

nice little nest egg. You've heard, "Laugh now, cry later," right? That's the simplest adage of what it means to have regrets. The person who gobbles up the menu at the local fast-food joint, avoids fruits and vegetables, and is a couch potato will eventually pay the cost with health issues. The person who spends frivolously, gobbles up all their wants, and foregoes a budget will ultimately pay the cost in retirement.

Your budget should be congruent with your goals for retirement. Make your finances anti-fragile, and you win. The weightlessness you should feel once you've moved all your chess pieces on the board should be liberating.

You want to take a quick jaunt? Budget! Your BFF is getting married? Plan and budget. A budget is an invaluable tool that helps you summarize and prioritize your spending. It's money management at its most basic level and gives you financial clarity to plan ahead. If your budget is accurate, you can plan for a deficit or budget to avoid one.

Cheap Girls Club focuses on saving for retirement, which should be your ultimate goal. However, a goal within a goal is possible if you (say it with me) budget! Whichever budget method you chose, you should always track your spending and set your bills on auto-pilot to help streamline your finances.

Below are tools designed to help make budgeting quick and relatively easy. And, lastly, use the financial apps and websites. I cannot say enough that these tools are equalizers. These resources crunch the numbers for you, giving you a full picture in black and white for your understanding. Don't belabor or stay up late nights writhing your hands together, losing hair and sleep. Remember, you got this!

Free Personal Finance Coach

◊ Penny app is chat-based, tracks your finances, and helps you strategize.

Financial Software

◊ Mint.com
◊ PersonalCapital.com
◊ Filethis.com
◊ Learnvest.com offers a paid subscription for a combination of human and algorithmic analysis and planning.
◊ Wally.com is an app that helps you balance and analyze your spending

Meditative Minutes

Budgeting should be a regular part of your day like brushing your teeth or getting dressed. It should be instinctual and deliberate. Think about how your ancestors had to budget using old-school methods—pencil, paper, calculator—and then meditate on how fortunate you are to have modern financial tools at your fingertips. Then use 'em.

Cheap Girls Club Oath

Now that you've learned how to save more, create a budget, and manage your financial portfolio, remember to stay positive. A budget isn't punishment; it's power. It will serve you well to believe that.

Chapter Eight

Minimalism Is the Holy Grail of Financial Freedom

I've studied friends and associates with a handle on their finances. It's not that they had no problems; they just had no money issues. These people weren't rich in the economic sense, but they were leading rich, full lives. They had all they needed and desired. They traveled, ate great food, and had healthy social lives.

One lady I knew, Renee, wore a pair of black jeans and tennis shoes each time she came over to my home. If we met for dinner, she'd wear the same black jeans, and the sneakers were replaced with a pair of heels. Renee was a minimalist. She didn't dump her money into clothing, furniture, luxury cars, or dream homes. She loved to be outdoors, connecting with people. Renee and her husband lived nomadically, so it was difficult to hold on to stuff. That's where she found fulfillment, not through possessions but through people and experiences.

Another great example is a couple I met, Joshua and Angelina. When they say opposites attract, I am not sure that's entirely accurate. There needs to be a commonality, a cohesiveness to go the distance with relationships. Both husband and wife were cheap minimalists. All their furnishings were from thrift stores or secondhand from family.

They shared one closet, and there was lots of remaining space. Both had bicycles, and they shared a used car for long trips and heavy loads. Joshua and Angelina owned several rental properties and worked part-time in fields of their liking to cover healthcare. Their assets were more than their liabilities, and therefore they were wealthy. The duo invested for retirement and had a bright outlook for their financial future. The couple tried to mentor me on finance, but I wasn't ready. I couldn't receive their guidance because the wants in my life were too powerful and had a hold on me.

In my own time, I realized that material things did not bring a measured level of joy. The rewards were volatile, fleeting, and unable to sustain the high I received when I made a purchase. My metamorphosis happened gradually, as the hibernation of a bear. Eventually I wanted less. Therefore I saved more.

At first, the excess became a nuisance. The summers would bother me most. Looking at hoards of winter clothes during the hot summer months was vexing. And guess whose new designer bag was suddenly an old designer bag? Then the reverse would happen. Spring cleaning became a monumental task with a "get-rid-of-the-clutter" goal. And I would. I would give away one quarter of the old and then replace it with half of the new. For all this excess to appear normal, I needed to keep the clutter neat and organized.

Soon, it wasn't just about clothing. It became about floor mopping. How many floors needed to be mopped per week in my home? Then there were the windows, the baseboards, and the lawn mowing. When housekeeping becomes a full-time job, and you already have a full-time job, you have to bring in the professionals. And what if you can't afford to source things out? Suddenly, you realize it's time to reevaluate what's going on, only to conclude that the house was too big to begin with.

Yup, it's like that. All these headaches occur when you are abundantly wrapped up in trappings.

How many hours of my life were spent doing maintenance? Maintaining what I already owned was a chore. I had to upkeep the upkeep. You have a lawn, you buy the lawnmower to upkeep the lawn, and then you must purchase parts and labor to upkeep the mower that's up-keeping the lawn. So you purchase a shed to maintain the mower that upkeeps the lawn. Then you must upkeep the shed that's storing the mower that upkeeps the lawn. This cycle never ends until you end it.

Initially, you welcome it. The larger the yard, the bigger the statement. Then that big ol' yard begins to bug you. You resent it. The cost to water it, fertilize it, aerate it, cut and trim it is high. And the frequency with which this has to be done is too demanding. The only time you can actually gaze at the lawn for more than a couple minutes is on the weekends, but the weekend is when you must groom it. So then you ask yourself, *What are you good for, lawn? Why did I buy you?*

You're doing all the work, have no time to enjoy it, and the only reward is when someone says, "Hey, nice lawn." And you smile. For a full two minutes, you feel great—accomplished. Yes, you have a lovely lawn and you're the envy of friends and neighbors alike, but at what cost? Is this lawn contributing to your life's purpose, or is it a time suck and financial drain?

You could get more enjoyment, health benefits, and reciprocation if you adopted a puppy, with which there is more interaction than grass. Now, this is an extreme example. Or is it? It depends on what fulfillment you will receive from your lawn. Should you plant a garden on your lawn? Gardening can be very therapeutic, which could very well justify the cost. Or if you plant fruits and vegetables and your garden brings forth a harvest, then two thumbs up. You are making your investment produce something of value. Reciprocity is the name of the Cheap Girls Club game. If there isn't an ROI, mentally or financially, let it go. Don't commit.

After feeling less than fulfilled by the things filling up my life and deducing how many hours of my life were spent working to pay for nonessentials, I realized it was time for me to do the big *M*. You've heard of the big chop, when a female cuts off **Minimalism keeps you consciously connected to your finances.** all her hair for a new beginning. Maybe it's because it's damaged, she's gone through a breakup, or she wants new energy. It's the same for minimalism. Your credit may be damaged, you must break up with creditors and bad habits, or you need new energy to start over.

Minimalism, as a tool, should ideally start with the young. We should teach our children before the world teaches them about consumer trappings and excess. However, it's never too late to adopt the concept.

I started off slow. I'm not advocating selling off all your worldly possessions, buying a piece of land, and living in a yurt. Any extreme is inherently unhealthy. Minimalism keeps you consciously connected to your finances. It has allowed me to subjectively look at the purchases I've made and objectively at the purchases I will make.

Once I realized I could release myself from all my excess baggage, my next focus was on consuming less. How long could I go without purchasing new junk? If I went six months without spending money on anything other than essentials, then I could reward myself with a bonus. Guess what? When bonus time came, there wasn't anything my heart desired other than the obvious Louisiana crunch cake, a lifelong mate, world peace, the world without prejudices, and liberty and justice for us all. All that to say I could not care less about a fancy coat or the new Yeezy's. I became laser-focused on getting my wealth up.

Purging myself of my belongings gave me a new perspective. Sell, Give, Donate, Trash, and Keep was how I compartmentalized my road to minimalism. That quickly got remixed to Sell, Give, Donate, and Keep. I own nothing trash-able. When I do buy, I buy the good stuff, and I believe that most things can be recycled or up-cycled. My first purge resulted in me giving away a lot of clothing, mostly items that no longer fit or were too young or old for my age. The Keep pile was still swollen. I had a hard time letting go of things because inside this woman was a little girl who hoarded things. A little girl who for so long went without and found it challenging to let go.

The Sell pile also remained on hold because it would take time to itemize and place things up for sale.

The Donate pile was easier to jump into. I love giving back, or giving in general. I would load up the truck and go to the nearest Goodwill or Salvation Army at least a couple times a year. When you donate to these nonprofit organizations, get a receipt for tax purposes.

Some time would pass, and I would still be up to my eyeballs in "keeps." My report card showed my grade in minimalism was a big fat F. I wanted it but somehow couldn't achieve it. So before I tried the process again, I meditated on why I wanted it for a few months. What was the end goal? Here's what I came up with, my truth.

Minimalism would help me in several ways. As a lifestyle, it would help curb spending. The less I needed, the less I would buy. It would also help me feel empowered. If there's not much in my home to steal, lose, break, or replace, then less worry. Less worry equals less stress—you get the picture.

Finally, there was the time management aspect of minimalism. Spending time maintaining my wants in life took away from what I now value as important, hobbies. If I wasn't putting fancy clothes in the cleaners, doing tons of laundry, placing furs in summer storage, or organizing what'd already been organized, then I could focus on my container garden, self-care, upcycling, DIY projects, meditating, reading, traveling, or conversing with friends.

I tried it again. Selling three-hundred-dollar jeans at a yard sale for ten bucks can be cathartic, but honestly, I had to silence the voice that kept telling me I should have never made such idiotic purchases. I was weighed

The less you need, the less you buy.

down by possessions and allowed these physical items to smother me. It was all so wasteful. You see something, you want it, you buy it. You're slaying—dressed to the nines on the imaginary runway—while cat-walking right to the poor house.

If you're under thirty, teetering between looking wealthy or building wealth, then take heed. Learn from my mistakes. I sold off 60 pairs of designer jeans and invested the cash in a stock. Clutter reduction felt good. Every other year I will have a yard sale for things that haven't sold. I have uploaded all my Sell category items to various online sites, and purged all the Give and Donate baggage I accumulated throughout the years. I didn't even realize that I owned multiples sets of dishes—I mean a kazillion sets of dishes! I had duplicate sets of books, paper and audio, books I had bought, thought I lost, so I bought again, only to find the original.

As my closets are thinning out, the takeaway is that I don't miss one thing. A single person shouldn't live in such surplus. Should you take the time to look around your home and evaluate the things you haven't worn in six months, haven't used in six years, or didn't even remember you owned, you could find buried treasures to liquidate and add to your savings account. Nowadays there are several resources to unload things you no longer have a use for.

Here are some sites to help you on your minimalism journey:

◊ eBay
◊ Letgo
◊ Amazon Marketplace
◊ Facebook Marketplace
◊ Craigslist
◊ Offerup
◊ Bonanza for specialty items
◊ Close5

Technology:

Cell phones, used electronics, tablets, and videogames can all be sold through these marketplaces.

◊ uSell
◊ Gazelle
◊ Decluttr
◊ NextWorth

Growing up, I thought the more you had on display for people to see and envy meant that you had your finances in check. For instance, if someone came over to your house and your closet was stocked full of clothes, it represented wealth. Cheap Girls know that the theory has been disproven. Tangible items shouldn't make the statement of wealth. Wealth is about how many commas you accumulate before you're ready to cash those chips in. Be cheap and intentional on how you spend what you've worked so hard to earn.

If you have faith in this method, you can focus on what truly has value, rid yourself of unnecessary surplus, find a purpose that supersedes material things, all while saving your money. After all, isn't that the end game?

 Meditative Minutes

The reason we should meditate on life-changing decisions is for clarity. Being in a place of stillness will silence the noise of your ego and allow you to receive the answers.

 Cheap Girls Club Oath

Take an oath to minimize your debt by being a minimalist. Your future and quality of retirement life will thank you.

Chapter Nine

Downsized

Downsizing isn't something you should haphazardly consider. Don't do it for Facebook likes or Instagram followers—*Look at me! I'm downsizing!*—only to be miserable once the fanfare has subsided. When you're in debt, living paycheck to paycheck, or have realized you're hoarding a lot of unused resources, it might be a good time to have this conversation.

Extreme downsizing is not for everyone, and you should test drive this car before you buy it. Have a sound mind and purpose before scaling back your square footage and trading off your worldly possessions. Focus on the fundamentals, and be realistic.

Think about how you're going to use your scaled down space. Let's say a couple with two children is looking to downsize from three bedrooms to one. The couple will use the living room as their bedroom, while the children share the bedroom. They may consider moving near a park to have outdoor space.

If a family likes to congregate in the living room or kitchen, they could focus on searching for something that might have a larger gathering room and less bedrooms, or vice versa. Are you leaving behind an in-ground pool that your children absolutely love? Try searching in neighborhoods with a YMCA or a public pool. Downsizing becomes more about which areas of the home you use most than how much square footage you could do without.

Things to Consider When Downsizing:

◊ Walkable neighborhoods
◊ Local and state parks
◊ Public transportation
◊ Public pools
◊ Bike trails

About four years ago the tiny house became the entire rave. Americans wanted to live debt-free with the freedom to change their locales according to their wants and desires. They could freelance or work seasonal jobs instead of committing to full-time employment. They could live off the land with container gardens, solar power, and composting toilets. Alternatively, they could purchase land and build their tiny home, complete with electricity, gas, and water—modern living, simplified.

Talk show host, author, comedian, and entertainer Steve Harvey had an opinion on this tiny-house trend. Mr. Harvey, who has featured his huge home on his talk show and speaks repeatedly of his wealth, allegedly found this to be overall small thinking. He allegedly said those tiny homeowners are stupid, had no faith, and had given up. I respectfully disagree. Not everyone wants to live in extravagance, even if they can afford it. Not everyone needs to flaunt wealth for everyone to see.

Steve Harvey is enjoying his new money, but to have a negative opinion about those with different dreams and resources is money-shaming. Some people were millionaires several times over before Steve entered that tax bracket, and they live on tiny boats in the South of France. Are they acceptable to Mr. Harvey because instead of a tiny house it's a tiny boat? They drink cappuccinos and go to art museums, and instead of an American accent, he hears something foreign. Are those millionaires stupid? Or are those people worthy of his respect? People with less debt have less clutter in their minds, and by default have less to worry about. Therefore, they can live more abundantly. #Facts.

The Cheap Girls Club will take our lead from the examples below. A few years back I read about the tech millionaire who sold his mansion and New York City apartment to downsize to a 400-sq.-ft. home.

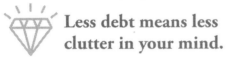 **Less debt means less clutter in your mind.** Was he thinking "stupid" or practically? He didn't wait for the world to dictate whether it was cool for millionaires to downsize or live a minimalistic life. He realized that less is more in a lot of instances.

The world will tell you that low cost is synonymous with inadequate. If you have a small home people feel that you're unhappy. A used car means you're in debt, growing fruits and vegetables means you're broke. However, billionaire Jeff Bezos, CEO of Amazon, still drives his 1996 Honda, billionaire Mark Zuckerberg drives a Volkswagen GTI, and billionaire Warren Buffet drives a Cadillac. I honestly believe we would never hear any of these philanthropist billionaires harping about the "stupid" people who've downsized or chose to drive a Honda instead of a Porsche.

In 2015, *The New York Times* ran an article on housing developers putting plans together to build micro-apartments to address the growing need for single-adult housing. These apartments, ranging from 260 to 360 square feet, are designed as affordable, private spaces for single men and women. Since then, the downsizing platform has gained traction, and micro-apartments are popping up all over Brooklyn and Manhattan.

Most middle-class Americans usually go through this cycle. They get married and incur housing debt around age thirty, give or take five years. By the time they're reaching retirement, the home is finally paid off. However, they're older now, and cutting the grass each weekend is less appealing. And guess what? That twenty-five-year-old roof has seen better days, and forget about the HVAC system. They look around at their large home with three to five bedrooms, and realize it's empty. The kids are gone, spread throughout different states, and the grandkids hardly come around. Walking up and down the steps to get a snack is a pain in the ass. Literally. The expense of maintaining your dream home after retirement invokes stress. They're over it. The days of showing off the pool are long gone. So they place the house on the market and downsize to an apartment—maybe a condo or co-op, or even a rental. Once they've come to the end of the road, they think, *Why was I so determined to own a home?* Society has us thinking it's a byproduct of the American dream. I know. I bought into that mindset too, only to long for the simplicity of my one-bedroom, 700-sq.-ft. apartment.

Downsizing will be met with criticism. It is not for the faint of heart. If you have an ego, check it at the door. Your decision will be dissected by others, mocked, ridiculed, and consistently judged. You will need thick skin.

At first, you'll want approval. You will want friends and family to cosign your decision. Next, you'll wrestle with your current and former life. You'll feel ashamed and want to prove to others that you made a sound decision. You'll go out of your way to let others know that you're happy, perhaps even laying the happiness on too thick. Then you'll be combative with those who want to continually remind you of what you had then and what you have now. During this transition, you'll continue to wonder if you made the right decision. Finally, things and emotions will settle down, and you will come to terms with the responsible decision you made as you tackle debt and realize that you are controlling your life, not allowing life to control you. Think before you allow others to have a say in your life, in your decisions, in your finances. If they aren't paying your bills, pay them no mind.

Downsizing isn't just about income or debt. It can also be for those individuals who are seeking change.

A few years ago on a flight, I met a woman preparing to go abroad to open a yoga studio. The woman said she lived with her parents until she was thirty. She saved a ton of money, married her husband, and

 **Trappings are entrapment.**

they bought their first home outright. She and her hubby were cheap by nature and had done very well by being so. They held the home for ten years before they chose to sell and downsize. They made a profit from the sale of their home and used a small portion of the profit to purchase their yoga studio. The couple planned to use sweat equity to make the studio ready for its grand opening. We had a rich conversation about downsizing and minimalism. Later I meditated on what I had learned. Trappings are entrapment. They trap you into thinking you need them. They trap you into worshipping them. They trap you into an inflated ego.

Steps To Take To Downsize:

1. Determine how you use your current space.
2. Choose your new property based on those needs.
3. Measure your new square footage and then your furniture to see what fits.

4. Assess your belongings and place a sticky note with either SELL or BYE on the items you want to get rid of. You will need to go through every inch of your home. Most people do not realize how much stuff they've accumulated throughout the years. Kitchen drawers, closets, under each bed—it all needs to be evaluated and categorized.
5. Donate/trash all the BYE items.
6. Sell as much stuff as you can.
7. Do another walkthrough. This time be more aggressive. You might find that you've tried to hold onto clutter for emotional reasons. Ten boxes of finger painting from your children who are now adults should go. Concert ticket stubs and memorabilia from your favorite band should probably go as well.
8. Organize.
9. Move.

*Depending on the size of your new downsized space, you might want to consider multifunctional furniture like a sofa bed, mirror/wardrobe, drop-leaf tables, collapsible trays, or stackable tables.

It is clearly within the nature of some mammals to exploit those in weaker positions. When you are your most vulnerable, the predators will attack. Cheap Girls are fearless and, in the face of any financial hiccup, should be brave. If you had to downsize your child from private to public school, most would never let you forget that. So when your house turns into an apartment, keep your head up. You are the CFO of your life. Remember, Do you, babe! and give the middle finger to naysayers.

Should you need help, there are property downsizers and professional organizers available. Look in your local area. NASMM

(National Association of Senior Move Managers) helps seniors and families when it's time to downsize.

 ## Meditative Minutes

Downsize before being downsized. That way you don't relinquish your power. Clear your mind, meditate, and make an informed decision.

 ## Cheap Girls Club Oath

If your finances are feeling the pinch, then downsizing should be a consideration. You're apprehensive, have reservations, and the experience could be both the most beneficial and terrifying thing of your life. Only allow those involved to have a say in this decision.

Chapter Ten

Handle Your Business

There's a pretension that comes with the title of business owner. I have witnessed firsthand business owners lose their minds day one of launching a company. Their hubris lacks charm, and they forget to be graceful as they shove their accomplishments down our throats. Many people on social media list "entrepreneur" on their profiles and advertise an entrepreneurial life that promotes private jets, popping bottles, and five-star everything. This is a lifestyle that only a small percentage of people will acquire, and a reasonable person should be able to discern between fact and fantasy.

But these over-the-top depictions help bolster fallacies and illicit haters to hate. The moment people realize you are the boss, a tiny seed of resentment appears to take root. Each day they must get up and punch a clock, the seed of resentment is watered. Each time a supervisor pisses them off, they think about the imaginary beautiful life you must live. They don't realize that the struggle is real for large and small business owners, alike. You have no company paying for your healthcare; you *are* the company responsible for paying for healthcare. Human Resources doesn't give you a packet that outlines your 401(k) or pension. You're solely responsible for that too.

When you sit down to have a meal at a restaurant, everyone at the table assumes you are charging the bill to the company. Again, you *are* the company, and these are not business-related meals. There are so many occasions early on when I started my business when no one reached for the restaurant bill. They were all drunk off the fact that they knew someone with a company and assumed it would be like the movies, where you charge it to the corporate account.

I remember going to the zoo with friends from out of town. I had opted last minute to pick up the tab. There were six of us, and I handed the cash to one friend while I went to pay for a locker. When we all met by the lockers, my friend came running toward me with the receipt.

"Here, I kept this for your records."

"What records?" I asked, perplexed.

"So you can write this off on your business taxes?"

Cute and well intentioned, but misinformed. I took the receipt and tossed it in the trash with the locker receipt. I would have given her a quick lesson on how you don't try to write off a personal day trip to the zoo with friends on your business taxes, but I knew it would go in one ear and out the other. It's easier for people to believe that when you're picking up tabs that it's a win-win, to clear their conscience. Instead of appreciating the kind gesture, they must muddy up the waters by choosing to believe you did it not out of kindness, but because you will make the government eat it.

I have witnessed people call themselves bosses, yet have no business or employees. Moguls, yet never closed a deal. Everyone wants to be a big deal, but that comes with a hefty price. People think that somehow you received the golden ticket. You have a title or position that seems elusive to them.

For me, there are two ways to handle your business. You can get a handle on your bills and finances, concentrate on growth, and focus on quality assurance. Another way is to play the role of being in business, be showy and egotistic, pick up checks, and smugly announce, "This is going to the corporate account," giving folks the reality show they are craving. The latter isn't my shtick.

Before starting my business, I owned a three-bedroom colonial home, a one bedroom co-op apartment, and two vehicles, one used and one new, all acquired through good old-fashioned hard work. For years I worked two, sometimes three jobs. At one time in my life, I worked full-time as a legal assistant and full-time at the Internal Revenue Service. At another time, I was a full-time legal assistant and working full-time with mentally challenged adults. These jobs destroyed my sleep pattern, which maxed out at four hours per night.

In 2002, I opened my company. When I opened my business, I honestly did not understand what I was doing. I had passion, drive, and determination, but what I didn't have was a business plan. I did not put in resignation letters to my paralegal and health assistant jobs until late 2003. So for twenty months, I was working three jobs. Monday through Friday, from 10:00 a.m. to 6:00 p.m., I worked in lower Manhattan as a paralegal; from 11:00 p.m. to 7:00 a.m., I worked on Ronkonkoma, Long Island; and on the weekends I drove state to state doing book signings and promoting my works. I had also opened a bookstore, but I wasn't putting in any hours.

I was invested in something, but couldn't put my finger on why I was so driven. I can say I wasn't working this hard to be famous. I'm an introvert by nature. And I can say I didn't visualize being wealthy. I was too pessimistic back then to even remotely consider it a possibility. My single reason for working twenty-hour days was that I did not want to be poor again, and those were thoughts from a practical person. Back then I paid everyone first—book manufacturer, sales representative, publicist, Con Ed, office supplier, freight and fulfillment companies, the lease on the bookstore, staff—a buffet of bills. I would then take my share from whatever was left over. If at the end of the month the till was empty, then I received nothing. I kept thinking it would all make sense in the end.

For approximately a decade, my company experienced growth through the economic downturn of 2008. We had growth through various legal attacks and continued to have growth even when we scaled down our roster. However, what good was monetary growth when I was bewildered about money management? Our revenue was impressive, but the margin was small.

It took ages to realize that my business was financially flourishing. Each time I would sit down with my CPA and go over my profit and loss report and my balance sheets, which would spell out the revenue and margins, I would always be stunned at the gross. "Where did the money go?" I would want to know.

It wasn't a situation where I was paying myself top dollar; I kept my salary slightly above what I earned as a paralegal. One CPA said I should think about increasing my wages, equivalent to someone in my position as a publisher. What I didn't admit to him was that I couldn't—maybe *shouldn't* is more accurate. I knew that if I increased my salary, then it would be more money for me to misuse and not necessarily on myself. I also deduced that it would not be wise to give myself the increase, pulling substantial cash flow from the business. My needs were met.

Instead of creating a business plan or hiring a financial advisor, I continued on my path as a spendthrift. There were no weekly meetings where we went over our budget. The money came in, the money left out. I was spending top dollar on printing, shipping, freight, storage, bubble wrap, tape, and a host of essentials at premium cost. There were so many issues I would always table for the following day.

Throughout the years I had problems with production, lack of workforce, inadequate machinery, and a sales manager who over-promised and under-performed. I had a publicist whose agreement included a fixed rate plus expenses: car service, food allowance, hotel and flight reimbursement, postage, telephone, and messenger service. These expenses consistently plagued my day-to-day operations. I was a boutique publishing house masquerading as major. There was an expectation I allowed to be put upon myself, and the justification was this is the "entertainment" business. This is what "we" do.

Somehow each conversation, questionnaire, or Dun and Bradstreet inquiry would end with, *How much does your company gross?* Or, *How many books has your business sold?* The question is obvious in its intent. It's structured to fleece you. Even when applying for a rewards card to buy office supplies they have you indicate what your company earns. And each quarter I would get a call from the office supplies sales manager trying to solicit an increase in buys.

The sales rep, publicist, manufacturer, lawyer, insurance company, and fulfillment company all feel that your business's finances are for public consumption. Why? Because they are handling their business, and I realized that I would do well to do the same. Why does a sales rep, publicist, or lawyer want to know your company's gross sales receipts? So they can bill you according not to the cost of the job that they've done, but at what they feel you can afford. The difference is staggering.

So there I was, continually putting out fires, worrying about the distractions, and not focusing on the root causes. I was incensed when the inflated bills would come through. I reasoned that it was simpler to pay the bill than to spend endless hours in dispute. I became a slave to everyone else's greed.

It took a while to realize that my independent publishing house was helping to make other people rich. The last fiscal quarter of each year, I would receive a slew of letters informing my business that beginning January 1, costs would rise. Some costs would increase one hundred percent, others less. The thing about publishing is there is an industry standard. While prices continued to grow, the retail price on a mass market, trade paperback, or hardcover book didn't see a corresponding increase, so the increased costs aren't passed along to the consumer; the business has to eat it.

Once I sat down and reviewed my finances—no expert, just me—I felt I had to change how I looked at money. I knew I could do it because I understood my business, and I cared about my future and my bottom line. I called account after account and renegotiated the terms. If the company didn't want to move the needle in my favor, then I took my business elsewhere. Remember, everyone has a competitor, even if you don't know it.

I looked at all the cash guzzlers and started there first. I found heavy duty shipping tape for 18% less at a competitor, switched manufacturers and saved 22%, shaved 5% off freight, let go of the sales representative and publicist, and a whole host of bills were lowered. You may see larger companies taking proactive measures to cut costs. One obvious method is paperless statements, which eliminate printing and postage costs. It's the go-green initiative that lessens our carbon footprint in the world

 Push back on costs that are unreasonable or not competitive.

while saving the company money. Remember, a company is never too big to save.

Even if you don't own a company, perhaps you're self-employed or freelance, the logic still applies. Don't just accept that you can't get quality for a lower price. Nowadays, I push back on all costs that seem unreasonable or aren't competitive. Each year I look for savings and either reinvest the capital back into the company or throw it at debt, whichever is applicable.

About five years ago I hired an independent contractor to do some freelance work for my company. She's an intelligent woman and wanted to make sure she was seen as such. Her e-mails were lengthy and chock-full of everything from prose to politics, but she never got around to handling business. Each deadline would be blown with the obligatory "dog-ate-my-homework" type of excuse. I think she was really oblivious that blown deadlines were unacceptable and a surefire way to not be rehired. A week or two before major holidays, I would get an e-mail from her asking if I needed additional help. To lighten the load for other contractors, I gave her another shot. What did she do? She missed the deadline again. And not by a day or two, or a week or two. She would blissfully hand in projects twelve weeks past due and then ask for another one.

When you handle your business in this manner, cash flow issues are inevitable. No one wants anything that's unreliable. Should you land an account that pays on time with reasonable terms and consistent work, you don't mismanage that account; you respect it and scout for more that are similar.

If you own a small business, there may be a time you have cash flow issues. This is vexing because you not only have your income but the salaries of your employees to stress over. That's a lot of pressure placed squarely upon your shoulders, and when your net 90 days billables turn into net 180, reconciling your books is frustrating.

If accounts receivable is often hard to collect, there is a remedy called factoring, where the business sells their open invoices to the factor (third party) at a discounted rate. Companies factor accounts receivable for a host of reasons from payroll, expansion, unforeseen expenses, litigation, and day-to-day cash needs.

About four years ago out of frustration and aggravation, I began the process of selling one account receivable to a factor. I had been having collection issues with one distributor for the past five years and was feeling the pinch. Our account was on a net 90-day pay schedule, which means each invoice was due ninety days after shipped. However, the distributor was two years in arrears. This distributor controlled sixty percent of our inventory, and if they ever closed or filed for bankruptcy, then it would cripple, if not end, my company.

A long paper trail outlined numerous failed attempts to collect. Then one day I received an e-mail stating that the business had been sold and a new corporation would be paying their debts. Within five weeks we were paid in full. What I didn't know then was that the distribution company had been sued twice in those five years and undoubtedly used our monies to stay in operation. Those firms they owed, including mine, essentially gave this company an interest-free loan for 24 months.

My story had a happy ending, but in business, it doesn't always end well. There were several times it did not end with favorable terms for my company. Companies, including Borders and Waldenbooks, filed bankruptcy without reconciling their debt to my business.

I feared if I pushed too hard then I would sever my deal with a powerhouse. Imagine you bake pies and land a sweet deal to have your pies sold nationally in Big Time Foods (fictitious name). Big Time Foods is helping your pies become a brand name. Each month you get purchase orders and then sit around waiting to be compensated. They pay you a little, just enough so you can manufacture, make payroll, and barely cover essentials. You can't expand because you have no money. Your debt piles up and you do what most would—you harass their accounts payable department, who could give two flying monkeys about you or your "small" company. You're treated disrespectfully by the accountants because they are used to dealing with brand names like Pillsbury or Nabisco. The staff is all wondering how your pies got in anyway, when they have Entenmann's and Patti LaBelle. This was what I was dealing with.

When I look back, I handled that situation in the worst possible way, even though the outcome landed in my favor. I allowed myself to be bullied into submission out of sheer fear. I didn't know my worth. I was so grateful I had made it into the club, I took the mistreatment. Had the shoe been on the other foot and I had owed the distribution company what they owed me, I would have not only gotten threatening letters from a tough-talking attorney, I would have been sued swiftly.

This is a lesson that I do not care to repeat, but should that situation befall me again, I will unequivocally handle my business. A Cheap Girl needs her money to handle her business!

In business, if you ever feel resistance from a client, company, firm, or distributor, maybe you should consider factoring at the first sign of trouble. Remember, even giants fall hard.

Another cautionary practice is to keep a lawyer on retainer. That is the most valuable decision you will ever make. I will elaborate further later, but save it at the forefront of your mind. This will save you money should you ever encounter litigious individuals, protect your assets, and give you peace of mind, knowing you have someone you can trust on board.

Meditative Minutes

Meditate for a moment on the vision you have for your business. What does it look like? Consider areas where you can realize increased savings you might not have thought about before.

Cheap Girls Club Oath

Handle your business, or it will handle you. If you think you don't have time to look for ways to save, then get used to getting bilked. Predators are everywhere—in business, in relationships, in families and friends. Pledge to take a hands-on approach to cutting costs in your finances, whether personal or business.

Chapter Eleven

Cash Flow

*I*f you continue to have more month than money, then you should make cash flow a priority. I did. For me, my spending was out of control. I could sneeze and spend a few hundred in a day and not remember any purchase. At the end of the month, I could never account for the debt. Each year, after fixed and variable expenses, I would blow through my net salary on nonsense and then promise that the following year would be different. When I had zero dollars in my bank account, I would pay with credit for business and personal expenses.

Emotional spending, lack of budgeting, and fractured infrastructure ate up my capital. Everything at ground zero was dysfunctional. The writers continually missed deadlines, editors were overworked or under qualified, and my manufacturer raised the prices while lowering the quality. I vacillated between being an author and a publisher, and I needed to be committed to one area if I wanted to succeed while the company was in its infancy. The business was suffering from all directions. Overall, I was ineffective. I became

 Cash flow is the top reason companies go out of business.

a statistic, because cash flow is the top reason companies and sole proprietors go out of business.

A word of caution: Don't use savings to springboard you into frivolous spending. I know the pattern. You see that you have X amount of money in your account and you get spending fever. You've been eyeing a new MacBook Pro, but your Dell is working fine. They're advertising the latest version of QuickBooks Premier, but your earlier version is adequate to accommodate your needs. Do you make the purchase? Not if you're a Cheap Girl. If you're still vacillating between wants and requirements, be honest with yourself.

Self-employed, small business owners, and freelancers do not have the benefit of job security or benefits of any kind. They don't get paid for sick days, personal days, or holidays, and must pay out of pocket for health insurance. With so much pressure you cannot afford to not have discipline.

Each election, Robin Hood politicians promise to lower the deficit without raising taxes. Hogwash. The campaigns to make the rich pay their fair share and provide government funding for the poor are misleading. To lower debt, they usually cut programs for the poor, and raise taxes on the middle class, not the wealthy. That's the formula! Yet, I'm saying use that same approach.

Beef Up Your Cash Flow

◊ Set your goal. In this case, Cash Flow. You can start with a small goal of 5% and then gradually increase. Ideally, 20% should be on your radar.

◊ Budget.
  o Filethis.com is a cool app to sync your current, and up to 3 years past statements to your phone, send you due payment alerts, and track your bills.
◊ Cut costs. Go ham on all those unnecessary perks that you could live without.
◊ Consider raising your fee, but only if it's justifiable and competitive, but not at the detriment of losing any clients.
◊ Look for supplemental income.
◊ Very importantly, pay your quarterly taxes. Cheap Girls do this to avoid interest and penalties. Fees eat away at your cash flow and earned income.

Stability Matters

Freelance and self-employment start off blissfully. You have only to worry about yourself, no boss, no employees. You make your work hours, yet know that you must be disciplined. You work from home, often in your pajamas with a hot cup of Joe in unlimited supply. There are conference calls, Skype meetings, and your closest friends secretly envy your life. You're a smart, resourceful go-getter. You find clients and you gain accounts. Slowly there's expansion. The money comes in, and at the end of each year, you feel accomplished. You're doing things your way, and it feels perfect.

This is great until there's a lull. Some of your clients leave you for someone equally qualified but at a lower cost, or can no longer afford your services. Perhaps some of the firms went out of business owing you a large sum of money. Whatever the reason, there's been a dip in your income, and you recognize that you're not prepared.

You think about retirement and healthcare and lack of accrued vacation pay and realize there's instability in self-employment. Slowly, you begin to panic. How do you make ends consistently meet when your income is inconsistent?

If you're a self-employed freelancer or a small business owner, look at your income like the stock market. Your earnings can be volatile. The fluctuation makes it difficult to budget, but not impossible. Budget for bad days just as one with a steady income would. Just like the stock market, monitor your projected cash flow accounts daily if not weekly. If a particular stock in your portfolio is doing well and others not so great, then you should rebalance. When your accounts receivable is in the black, take the surplus to rebalance your checkbook. The savings should be set aside to stabilize the months your business could expect a lull.

If you can admit to yourself that you are not to be trusted with money—have no shame, knowing your shortcomings is half the battle—then pay in advance. An example of this is if you're a freelancer or self-employed and you have four accounts lined up the first 90 days of the year. If budgeted correctly that income could cover your fixed (essential) expenses for six months. Pay those bills up front for the six months. Should you either not secure new accounts or find supplemental income (which we will discuss more below) you will have the security of knowing that all your essential bills are covered. I know a lot of freelancers, small business owners, and self-employed individuals who use this method to stagger cash flow.

Let's say your rent is $500/month, you work from home, and an account comes through that pays $2,000.

1. $200 - Pay yourself first—ten percent off the top into savings.

2. $1500 - Pay three months' rent (fixed expenses) to your landlord in advance.
3. $300 - Send the utility companies a lump sum to alleviate undue stress.

Small business owners who lease office space do this too. I've known some to pay a year in advance on a lease due to inconsistent funds. Now if you have discipline, the money could sit in your account and earn a small percentage of interest, which is favored.

Here are suggestions for stability and expansion:

1. Upload your resume to freelance job sites:
   ◊ Upwork.com
   ◊ Indeed.com
   ◊ Guru.com
   ◊ Simplyhired.com
2. Create a business profile on LinkedIn, Facebook, Twitter, any and all social media outlets and tout your professional skills to solicit potential clients.
3. Contact your customers at the end of each year and ask for a projection of work for the forthcoming quarter, and then repeat. This is imperative because it helps you budget and guesstimate cash flow.

Having steady cash flow for those in unstable positions is crucial. If you don't want your company's Internet shut off a couple times a year, or if you dread past due notices in the mail, then work on stretching your cash.

Meditative Minutes

We all try to choose a career path that will either bring us fulfillment or job stability. Some people are fortunate to get both. If you've stepped out on faith and are pursuing your dreams—entrepreneur, freelancer, artist, actor, or singer—and you run into cash flow issues, meditate on the "why" of it all. Not why you're having money issues, but why you love your career path. Let those positive feelings cancel out any negative voices that may arise.

 ## Cheap Girls Club Oath

The tradeoff with the blissful independence of self-employment is uncertainty. You always must think three moves ahead and grind. The moment you stop being resourceful, get lazy, or let fear paralyze instead of motivate you, leads to you hanging an Out of Business sign around your neck like an albatross. Stay motivated. Stay resourceful. Stay Cheap. Stay about your business!

Part 2

Spend Less

Chapter Twelve

Valuable Lessons from Debt

I have long believed that what is meant to happen, will. Every act, decision, and positive or negative thought is a roadmap to your fate, good or bad. I've explained how I started my company. Let me explain what I had to do to keep it.

You already know how I found myself in debt before I turned twenty-one. My grandmother would always say, "The postman always rings twice," so I have never fully subscribed to finality. Somewhere in the deep recesses of my brain, I would think, if this happened once, could it happen again? I would always proceed not cautiously but hesitantly. After the rental car debt, I began a cycle of going in and out of retail therapy debt. I had to recognize my spending triggers and take the song off repeat. If the rental car debt was the flood, this new debt was the tsunami.

At the height of my business success, I had to defend it against two separate civil lawsuits, skillfully filed within weeks of each other by two allies in federal court. The process was arduous. There was mediation, financial disclosure, motions, countermotions, threats, more threats, settlement requests, and settlement refusals. That's stage one.

Lawyers tell you early on, in civil situations, both sides will lose something. I knew long before it got ugly that the only winners would be the attorneys. Law is structured to have that as a rule, with very few exceptions. For three plus years, everything I laid my eyes on I had to fight for. My opposition wanted it all. I mean, they didn't want me to be left with a crumb. When your lawyers start asking things like—"Do you want to settle? How much insurance does your company carry? How much liquidity can you get your hands on?"—you understand quickly that you are in this alone.

Deals are allegedly made that you are not privy to, numbers are allegedly scribbled on pieces of paper, and attorneys allegedly jot down how much they would like to make off your case. If their daughter has an upcoming wedding, guess who just paid for it? Your lawyer just decided to join that new country club, that's added to your bill under "research" and "meeting." It's all billable if entered correctly. During this time my company had to go through an IRS audit covering three years, and two more individuals sent legal letters threatening to sue. I tell you, I was up against an army.

In stage two, I had to go through the process of discovery, more motions, interrogatories, depositions, exhibits, more settlement talk, and if all those things failed to foster an amicable resolution, then trial. The Supreme Court judge who heard the case had to make a decision. Wait, it's still not over. The case now went before a magistrate judge to decide on damages. And there was still room for an appeal. During all of this, I felt my evidence was irrefutable. I had the receipts (e-mail exchanges, executed agreements, letters, memos, and canceled checks) all along, but no one wanted to button this ordeal up swiftly—not when there was money to be made.

As the litigation proceeded, the Internet chatter increased. I never allowed the noise to seep in. I remember thinking, *Nobody cares*. And I am one nobody, so the opposition tweeting about this war to a few thousand Twitter followers was fruitless. It wasn't strategic. The hateful tweets were supposed to provoke a reactionary rebuttal. But silence was my weapon of choice.

If you think that if you're sued then all you have to do is sit back and send your lawyer(s) checks each month, I can tell you that wasn't my experience. I don't know how I remained sane. Each week there was a new list of dizzying demands all designed to make me scream, "Uncle!" Earlier I told you that I was an organized hoarder. I keep everything down to the smallest piece of paper. But digging through nine years of financials looking for something you know is bullshit would be vexing to anyone. And I call bullshit on it all. It was a game of how high and how often they could make me jump. Had I shown any sign of weakness, fatigue, or passivity, then I would be working at your local fast-food drive-thru today.

I reflect on Steve Jobs and Apple. Building something from the ground up and having outsiders who didn't contribute a dollar to the startup, an idea to the vision, or time in the management profit off what you nurtured and developed is a fierce motivator. No one *gave* me anything. I didn't intern at a publishing house, have an associate editor as my mentor, or hobnob with New York's literary elite. Everything I have I earned. Daddy didn't give me an interest-free loan of a million dollars, venture capitalists didn't lend me the seed money, and I didn't get an inheritance from a relative. I worked, sacrificed, and worked some more.

So, two court cases, two litigation threats, and an IRS audit later, I tried to get things back to normal. This was a four-year ordeal from the inception to the end, and I was drained. Do you know how a beat dog will flinch anytime there is movement? That was me. My soul wasn't at peace. My "Spidey senses" told me to not exhale yet. Everyone said it was over and that I could now relax and focus on rebuilding. I had an upcoming birthday three months later, and although I normally don't celebrate my born day with fanfare and pomp and circumstance, I decided to throw myself a three-day pinky-raised, hoity-toity celebration. Why not? I had earned some R & R.

After my birthday party, I traveled to Italy: Milan, Venice, Lake Cuomo, and Verona. I then flew back to my little cove on the beach before circling back home. I should have felt victorious, renewed, and invigorated, but something was bugging me. That something came eight weeks later. Cue the doom and gloom theme music!

Let me set the stage. I had a morning flight back home from a trip to audition for a TV gig about women in publishing. My cousin-like friend, Pam, had set it up. I was so nervous because television isn't in my wheelhouse. In fact, it's far removed from it. I woke up around five, and by seven I refreshed my smartphone to see a stomach-churning letter from the same attorney and plaintiff who had just lost a federal case against my company. They were taking a second bite at the apple.

Here we go again! I thought. *Good grief! Is there no one else? Does the attorney not have other clients?* The e-mail outlined several demands, but in a nutshell, it was extortion. My company was being ransomed. My livelihood was being held hostage by terrorists, and the only thing I could do was see it through to the end. While the case was being tried in a court of law, a large percentage of my titles were pulled, and threatened to be pulled from the shelves of ALL major retailers. Every brick-and-mortar store and distribution company that housed my titles were all served with cease and desist letters, and e-book files were pulled for leverage. If I can't sell books, I can't make money. If they could stop my cash flow, then they could ultimately strong-arm me into settling. It was a good play.

They wanted my publishing shelf life to have an expiration date. I felt like I needed to go lie down for a few years. This was a money grab. Everyone involved thought they were digging for million-dollar payouts. What I kept thinking was that this wasn't even real money they were after; I had crumbs on a table in the big scheme of things.

My entire business was teetering on a lie. If it's believed, I'm broke. If it's not, I'm in debt. Those were my choices. The evidence was undeniably in my favor in each case, yet I went through each costly process. There was a cluster of smaller evils all merging together like cancer cells to destroy the body (my company) and take me down. Some fuckery was going on, and I always suspected that the plaintiff's legal counsel was working with someone who was supposed to be on my team. I just could never prove it.

Again, there was a strategy, and the shakedown was well crafted. I felt like the most hated girl in my industry. Maybe fairly, maybe unfairly. But the show must go on. I had an appointment in two days to meet with producers, and in the interim I needed to seek new counsel.

My flight was filled with angst, but as if knowing my name, I knew I was a fighter. I was mentally weary, but there was strength I knew I had in reserves but was reluctant to dig that deep for it. I knew that if life kicked me, I would get back up. Walking through the fire and coming out OK on the other side doesn't mean that you still don't have to walk through the fire. Would I get burned? Absolutely. Would I die? Not from a lawsuit.

About one week into the latest suit, and I had already met with producers, consulted my attorney, the late Ken Thompson, to review the non-disclosure agreement, and was mentally prepared to be in a room full of women all vying for camera time.

My friend Pam, who had gotten me the audition, wasn't in the industry. She was a casual friend to a friend of a producer. Yes, six degrees of separation in full effect. She and I went out to lunch at this eatery we liked. The waiter took our orders, and our appletinis came.

Pam said, "So I see you don't want to discuss money." Her voice was slightly assertive, but I couldn't tell if I was reading too much into her tone.

I replied, "No, that's not true. We've already discussed the terms. What I said to you is that I am not going to have my attorney draw up your management agreement, pay for it, do all the heavy lifting, and then call you my manager. Ken has already reviewed the non-disclosure television agreement, and I paid his fees."

She glossed over that fact. "Well, I want twenty percent of the television deal."

"Again, done. Write it up. You know I'm not sweating this."

She looked me dead in my eyes and continued, "And I want fifty percent of your company, Melodrama. I want fifty percent of it, so let's talk about that!"

Her lips were pursed tightly together, and briefly, in the midst of all the emotions and thoughts swirling around in my head, I wondered, *What the F does she have to be angry about?* Either by nepotism or subterfuge, she thought she would get half my company. Seriously, half!

She continued, "Rick (her boyfriend) said that I'm a mogul (she's not). I'm doing big things and making big deals happen (never closed any deals)."

Jesus, grab the wheel!

Pam wasn't just a friend. Until that date, she was like family. Our families were family. She was a person I had known most of my life and had trusted not just with secrets but my finances. She had the PIN to all my bank accounts, for Christ's sake. She was privy to all my lawsuit drama, man drama, family drama, enemies north, south, east, and west and this was how she came to me? They say that the enemy will always come as a friend first.

I am not overly sensitive, but this was a delicate time. I was less than two weeks in the middle of a Drake back-to-back type of lawsuit and she wanted to destroy me. To defend myself in these suits cost more than a couple grand. This wasn't small claims court. These suits were costing exorbitant figures a pop, and they had just stopped my cash flow, so I was scrambling. I was vulnerable. And I was rocked to my core by her demand. Her behavior was so awful and so alien that I told her I was offended. We were speaking very different languages when it came to this television deal.

Here I am in a street brawl—brass knuckles and homemade shanks type of a situation—holding on to my company with bloody fingernails, and she was leveraging our friendship for money? I asked where she was when I needed start-up capital. Or penned my first book, or signed my first author, or was driving state to state for name recognition? Where was she when the first lawsuit was filed? Or the second? And now the third? Where were her sleepless nights? She did not place one investment coin into building my company and would not take half, a quarter, or a penny. Partners bring something to the table. She wasn't the talent, she wasn't the brains, and she wasn't the bank, so why would I need her as my business partner?

I didn't go to the audition. I quit the show that I wasn't yet hired for, and Pam and I went our separate ways. Adversity will always show you who your friends are. Pam, who at the end of each phone call, said, "Love you, Chris," was one of the cast of villains trying to dangle me over a balcony by my ankles and make me sign on the dotted line in blood. The veil is so thin between love and hate that the boundary quickly gets crossed. You readily mistake one for the other.

Pam's offer was unequal to the deal on the table. All she did was tell me about an audition that I had to audition for. She should have received a finder's fee, yet I was going to enter into a managerial deal which would have netted her 20% of my television profits. I had no problem with giving her 20%; however, she isn't a manager. A hustler, yes, but she's not a boss, she works for one. I would've had to pay for the agreement to be drawn up and manage my own career and company just as I'd been doing for the past fifteen years. Pythagoras, a Greek philosopher, believed a simple principle—greedy people will lose it all. Hard work is a value that dates back to biblical times. You sow first, and then you reap; it gets no more elementary than that.

I learned that so many people are seeking validation. Exposure and adulation are intoxicating and bring out the worst in folks. Pam wasn't asked to audition for the show, but leading up to my audition, she'd talk about what she would do when the camera panned her way.

"I told everybody that I'm taking acting classes because if a scene calls for me to cry, I'm crying!"

Yes, she was that far gone. She also kept saying she was coming in the room with me for my audition so she could have her camera time, but the cable network vetoed that. They told her she could come, but she had to wait in the lobby with the rest of the people taking acting classes to cry on a show they are not on.

That final lawsuit went on for two years before the gavel finally came down in my favor. And admittedly, I was spent. Six years of my life in court. When I needed someone to lean on, only one friend was there. He helped me get through the darker days when everyone else got ghost. The same people who ate off the company's profit, belched, and walked away from the table full never showed support, empathy, or concern whatsoever. My one genuine friend jumped in and just started swinging, helping me to fight a battle that wasn't his to lose or win. He showed me reciprocity.

With my friend, meditation, and prayer, I survived. I also learned you can't build through chaos. You can't grow or be creatively stimulated while going through turmoil, but the beauty and creativity that will spark once you've walked through and survived the fire is limitless. I have stories and knowledge for days. My best works have been written through pain.

The first situations were training wheels for me. When you figure out the rules of the house, you win. I mentioned in the Handle Your Business chapter, that if you're self-employed, an independent contractor, or a small business owner, you should always have legal counsel on deck. This should be done before you find yourself embroiled in a lawsuit. Sit down and interview as many attorneys as possible; some give free consultations, others don't. Use Google to research the attorney's losses and wins, the area of expertise, and the highest court in which they've argued a case. Do they settle more cases than they try? Get a feel of how their operation is run. Is it small and quaint? Are they an associate or a partner of a firm? Is their name on that marquee? I promise you all this matters. A smaller guy could be susceptible to backroom deals, and a partner of a firm could have a nasty habit of overbilling to sustain salaries. I now have someone on retainer with all the information about me others used against me in the past. Someone I can trust. Someone who will be lobbying for my company, not trying dismantle it.

So what did I learn from all this debt? While the third legal situation was unfolding, miraculously, I made the best decision of my business career through this fog and chaos. While reviewing my profit and loss statements, the costs to lease commercial space took a huge chunk of the budget. If only I owned instead of leased commercial space, I could save over six figures a year. That's a no-brainer, right? I guess for years I had no brain because it never occurred to me. It took years of unbridled legal battles to open my eyes. First, it was an idea, and then became a deep thought before manifesting into a reality. Well, let's just say that it's all about timing.

Thankfully, I was able to purchase and renovate a space. Honestly, the renovation kept me distracted. The building placed me on the trajectory to see a ROI within four years. Today, I am on my fifth year, and it looks like a smart business decision.

Like two bookends my debt began and ended from others. All the chapters in between were my doing, but at the end of the day as long as it had my name on it, it got paid. The lesson I got from this last bout with debt is that I had an unbelievable amount of strength that I didn't know I had. There were years of no relief.

Life can be like a videogame. You can't go to the next level until you go through some obstacles. And if you give up, then you'll stay stuck. Game over. I survived my worst nightmare, and I'm still here. Grinding. Creating. Living. Loving. Focusing on being cheap and debt-free. I've earned it. I've earned the right to exhale. And I want everyone to know that if I could find the tenacity, faith, and sheer willpower to muster up the strength to fight back, then so can you.

Here's What I Learned:

1. You should save for rainy days and create an emergency fund. Because shit really does happen. And it doesn't happen because you deserve it, you're an evildoer, or even reckless.
2. Ignoring debt, hiding from it, doesn't make it go away.
3. Debt doesn't mean you can play dead. You still must get up and work, eat, interact, and socialize. And when you think, "Why did I get out of bed today?" know that what you're feeling is temporary.
4. Being in debt forces you to grow up.
5. Good things can come from adversities.

Meditative Minutes

Good things do come from tragedies. Have you ever had something unspeakable happen and questioned why? You could still be searching for the answer or may never get one. Meditate on what good came from a tragedy and then give thanks.

Cheap Girls Club Oath

Anything could happen, any day, hour, or minute in your life. Take an oath to seek the lesson from each loss because there is one.

Chapter Thirteen

How Wealthy People Look at Money

Initially, I described how I worked three plus jobs for some years, and I bought my first two properties. When I was twenty-something, I could work three or four jobs, my body acclimated to the sleepless nights, and I moved forward with purpose. As I aged, sustaining that level of mental and physical exertion became that much more challenging. I didn't understand that the way I looked at money—making and spending—would only take me so far. I knew the fundamentals: You want X (house/car/boat), you work Y (hours/jobs). I was clueless when I moved onto Z (tax bracket). Back then I thought the more hours I worked, the more money I would earn, never considering the increase in my taxable income. When I opened my own company, my eyes widened at the possibilities, advantages, and disadvantages.

Revenue and assets were my plans for monetary wealth. I would get my income from working multiple jobs—an unsustainable plan—and buy assets to bring forth additional revenue, that I could sell for retirement. But what about all those years in between? The years when I am most active and have all my wits? Aren't those years equally important?

My goal for myself was to focus on a high salary, assets, and investments. I had the salary, the assets, and the investments, but I didn't feel rich. I was too soft as a landlord with my rentals, I was blowing my net salary on frivolous things, and I was investing in low-risk investments. I was playing it too safe, too early, when I should have been making strategic moves. I was playing tennis when I should have been playing tackle football.

I thought I was on my way to living the good life. But I was living in one of the most expensive states in America, New York, so a life of leisure was less obtainable holding down a nine-to-five. Working simultaneous jobs could take me from poor to middle class, but little farther. I would never be wealthy if I didn't reclassify how I earned, spent, and invested my money.

Difference Between Rich And Wealthy

I went from middle class (working a few jobs) to upper middle class (the start of my company) and at the five-year mark of my business became the government's definition of rich (grossing $500,000 or more/year). Yet I didn't feel rich. The government was taxing me roughly 35-39% per year, 10% of that was to New York State, and after operational costs, the net profits were slim. I could have well been some economist's definition of rich, but I was a long way from being wealthy. Why? Because I was still struggling with my finances.

Then I realized that I needed to be wealthy because rich is relative to your wants, needs, cost of living, locale, and domicile. Limitations are still placed upon the rich. You have a few million in the bank you can't go island-hopping, private jet taking, and making it rain down benjamins all day. But when you're wealthy, well, you could leave massive inheritances, have money to splurge, and hire top CPA and money management firms.

How Do The Rich Get Rich?

Start early

Generation X and Millennials speak of saving millions in the bank for retirement. This traditional thinking is most likely reachable by starting early and investing 10% of your annual income over the next 40 years into your retirement accounts.

Education

Being knowledgeable and well versed in your field is invaluable and profitable.

Make money while you sleep

Whether you've parked a portion of your income in a high yielding money-market account, or a certificate of deposit yielding 5% for example, it's all about compound interest accruing monthly or annually. Perhaps you've invested in rental properties or a commercial location, examples where you are making money in real time without putting in hours in the day. Your money is making you money. There is no greater feeling than at the beginning of each month to have your tenants deposit rent into your accounts or to look at your bank statements and see how much interest your money has accumulated.

My method was to sink my net income into capital that ultimately increases in value. I did this for two primary reasons: (1) I did not trust myself with my profits, and (2) it gave me the ability to profit twice off one asset[5]. I would profit off the monthly rental, and again once I sold the asset. This approach could lead to a robust, productive life, but not wealthy in any sense of the word.

How Do The Wealthy Get Wealthy?

Follow me on this and form no opinion until after you've digested my point. *Cheap Girls Club* and its movement focuses primarily on saving money, frugality, and then investing for retirement. Yes, that is the message. But between the lines, and I will spell it out here, I want so much more for us. Just clipping coupons, accruing modest amounts of cash, and buying a property or two won't make you wealthy. It's a good start, though. You can live an abundant, fulfilling life, but let's aim higher.

Doing the points in this book should be coupled with using your own noggin. I learned that I had to retrain my brain to think differently about money, and that was a process. With my mind now free of worrying about debt, pleasing people, and frivolous spending, I can dedicate my free time to being creative, proactive, and to enriching ideas.

Question: How can I make the most money with the least effort and least start-up costs? If you already have a platform in a particular field, grow your brand vertically with variations of the original product and then horizontally, a subsidiary or umbrella under the central hub. A key to success is making sure the growth is an authentic extension of yourself and your brand.

As an example, publishers have a book that they release as a hardcopy. That same title can grow vertically by printing it in paperback and then

---

5   To profit twice off each of my assets works because each asset was purchased all liquid; therefore bank interest for loans does not apply.

mass market to maximize profits. Finally, the electronic version requires the least effort and start-up costs. Same book, generating revenue from different avenues. To grow your brand vertically, a publisher might start a subsidiary. If you publish teen-literature, the subsidiary may focus on children's books; an extension of the central hub. Think about Dr. Dre, who is most known for making beats. An authentic extension of his brand was headphones. Therefore, Beats by Dre succeeded. If you knit hats and addition would be gloves. You already have the infrastructure in place; so the start-up costs should be minimal.

Secrets of the Wealthy

Barter

Most wealthy people use their contacts as leverage. Think politicians. If I do X for you, then at some point you must do Y for me. These business deals at dinner meetings and in boardrooms are commonplace among the wealthy. It transcends all industries, and from Wall Street to Hollywood, most barter.

Beware of fraud, though. A few years back I met a couple, and from day one I knew what they wanted from me. They didn't ask right away, but I was already on notice just waiting to see how they would structure their approach. They had a vast Rolodex of who's who and continually made empty promises to leverage X (the favor they wanted from me) for Y (connecting me with their contacts to further my career). Year after year, they dropped big names. Whoever was the new "it" person in Hollywood they allegedly were in contact with them, and perhaps they were. But all I kept thinking was, *Why aren't the same individuals they claim they could get to help me helping them?*

The American Dream

Ever wonder why so many immigrants come to America and create wealth when you've lived here all your life and are still living paycheck to paycheck? It's because they believe in capitalism. They come to America knowing that it's a wealthy country. Remember, money has no bias or prejudices. Money doesn't attach itself only to the educated or people of a specific race or social status.

Greed

All the things I used to despise—greed, materialism, selfishness, being CHEAP—are the traits and beliefs of the wealthy. They know that they're supposed to have housekeepers, and car service and five-star dining and living, and they set about to make that happen.

Mindset

Author Napoleon Hill outlined in his national bestseller, *Think and Grow Rich*, that building wealth is more a state of mind than anything else. Know that you will and can be wealthy and focus on how to make that happen.

Be Allergic To Broke

No, seriously, let's not play here. Wealthy people despise the thought of poverty and believe that all problems and grief stem from it.

Work Vs. Idea

Work can make you rich, while an idea can make you wealthy. You can *work* as a surgeon—let's say, a neurosurgeon, to up the ante—and be rich. But an *idea* such as Twitter, Spanx, or Facebook could make you a very *wealthy* person. Revolutionary ideas are limitless. Remember, an idea that generates wealth can sometimes happen overnight.

Education Ain't The Holy Grail

While you can get rich from higher learning, that isn't always true of the person looking to gain wealth. A lot of wealthy people are high school and college dropouts and have acquired vast sums of capital. They are acutely intelligent but mainly in specific fields. You will see hoards of business, economic, and spiritual books in their home, as they're always looking to self-educate.

Bet On Yourself And Win

You can work for someone and love the stability that your gainful employment provides, but a wealthy person will always bet on themselves. They have a winner's mind and can't see investing that into anyone other than themselves.

Don't Play It Safe

Most of us focus solely on living well and then retirement. The wealthy know that, if blessed, life could be long, so they look at the big picture. How can I make enough money to set me up for my present, future, retirement days, and set up my future generations?

Other People's Pie

The wealthy person knows that she need not use her own money to build her fortune. Making money to make money isn't necessarily the way a wealthy person thinks. I would be remiss if I didn't address credit. STAY away from funding your idea to get wealthy by using credit. Don't listen to wealthy rappers' lyrics to get you back into debt. This is the Cheap Girls Club, and we've reprogrammed our brains. The wealthy person knows about getting funding from outside sources, such as venture capitalists, investors, or partners. You have the idea, the associates front the funding.

Haves and Have-Nots

Wealthy people divide the world into two sections, the haves and the have-nots. They all congregate in the small, exclusive club. This is why you can see a wealthy racist billionaire playing golf with a wealthy non-white billionaire. Because the first color billionaires see is green. Money doesn't solve all issues of race, inequality, or global warming, but it helps tip the scales.

Love Your Career

The wealthy also pick what they like doing and then get wealthy doing it. Think Gates and Jobs, who both had a love for technology.

Wealthy people know that if you want more stuff, then you must make more money. It's not about focusing on what you can save that year, it is always about how much you can earn that year. That's how the wealthy look at money. You make six figures, how can you make seven? Wealthy people know there is always more where that came from and enough to go around for everyone who goes after it. America is in a 19 trillion-dollar deficit. No one is cutting down trees to generate that amount of cash, so there is an infinite sum of money to be earned not physically made. Money illustrates your worth. Are you worth a hundred thousand or a hundred million? **Ask yourself, how do you look at money?**

Ask yourself, how do you look at money?

Meditative Minutes

Take some time to meditate on your relationship with money. Is it precarious? Are you frustrated? Any negative thoughts about money can manifest into your day-to-day life experiences.

 ## Cheap Girls Club Oath

When I was a teenager, I was sad and downtrodden. I thought I would never gross a hundred thousand, and in order for me to see a million it would have to be through a husband's career, not mine. Life felt difficult beyond words. I placed limitations on myself and my future. However, there was a small voice inside, a voice that would not allow my light to completely dim. My late grandmother's words that encouraged a ten-year-old that she could be someone in life if she just applied herself repeated themselves to me throughout the years until I took heed. It took a while, but I persevered.

Take an oath that if you've placed any financial limitations on your life that you will release yourself from negative thoughts and beliefs. Tell yourself that you can be WEALTHY, each day of your life. Aim high, girls. I now think of ways to earn my first hundred million.

Chapter Fourteen

The Road to Hell

Why, why, why do we continue to help those less fortunate than us when they are in need? Why do we place others' financial obligations before our own? Why do we make these kind gestures only to receive resentment from the receiver? Good deeds, if not contained, could lead you down the road to hell.

For years, I listened to my cousin Blair whine about what she didn't have and what she never did, and I meddled in her life. I had a nebulous, nagging need to please the people around me that would kick in the moment someone needed help. I would take on a person's problems, do what was necessary to solve them, and they would peacefully go to bed at night. She gave the open invitation, but, you know, Blair never directly asked for a handout. There is an art form to getting what you want and being able to say, "I never asked you for anything."

My retort: "But you took it, though." *Sigh!* Show me a person who says "I've never asked you for anything," and I will show you a person who willingly takes what you give.

I vividly remember the shift. We were on vacation paid in full by numero uno, and one night I went to bed early. Blair stayed out and went to the casino with my money and lost. This irked me on so many levels, because I don't gamble and because she could have used her own money but chose not to. She had only brought one hundred dollars on vacation, and on the last day she purchased a gaggle of T-shirts for her friends and coworkers back home. Of all the T-shirts she had gotten on sale, not one was for me.

That vacation put me on notice, and I watched her movements carefully. The whole time she was on vacation, she posted pictures daily on Facebook, saying things like, "I had to take a much-needed vacation" and "Having fun in the tropical sun." She was in la-la land, brimming with excitement. Of the sixty-plus posts, not one post mentioned me. I wasn't tagged in any pictures. It was like I wasn't there. I didn't exist. My sole purpose was to pick up the tab. That hurt. You help people and you feel like you're playing a bigger part in someone's life, helping them obtain what often can be unattainable—a brief moment of happiness.

To add fuel to the flame, I went to her Facebook page to understand if this was a "me" thing. If I was being over critical of who she was at her core. Fundamentally, maybe she's a thankless person. If that's who she is, who am I to change her? Post after post she gave praise and adulation to those who offered her birthday wishes, frozen cakes, or an e-card. I felt gut-punched. I didn't like the way it made me feel, so I shut down. I didn't confront her. It forced me to scratch my head and wonder why she had no problem thanking everyone except me.

I don't know many people who would have said this out loud, but Blair did. I was all in my feelings one day and asked why she found it difficult to say "thank you" for the assistance I had given her. Her response was, "If you're doing something from the heart, you shouldn't need me to say thank you."

Well, damn. There was a pregnant pause because her statement was so succinct, that it placed the spotlight back upon me. Now it wasn't about her ungratefulness, it was about my presumed need to be lauded. While I wanted less attitude and an ounce of gratitude, her response challenged the "why" factor for me. That jarred me awake. You have FREE on the one hand and THANK YOU on the other as an exchange, and some people won't make the trade. Saying thank you, showing grace, sometimes is too high a price.

The following summer I took my two younger nieces on vacation. When I got back, I invited Blair to hang out with me and my nieces for the weekend at a water park and game arcades. That whole weekend the anger from her was seeping through her pores. Stern looks, curt remarks; she was all snippy and snarky, and I had no clue what was bugging her.

By Sunday morning she couldn't stand to be around me and exploded. Blair argued at me for the full day. The whole car ride I stared straight ahead while she went insane. I remained quiet, allowing her to vent. Later I found out that the subject was broached on why I had only taken my youngest nieces on the trip and not her too. She went on and on about how she was off for the July 4th weekend and could have gone yet I didn't bring her. Her last remarks were, "You know Chris is always trying to buy someone's love. She's a people-pleaser."

Come again? Was that what I'd been doing? Her actions, remark, and ingratitude were so astonishing that I am still coming to terms with it. When Blair lost her job, I hired her until she found a new one. She owed unemployment, I paid half her bill. She was in a small, unsafe apartment, I put her in a home and kept her rent at the same cost of her apartment for eight years and counting. Blair wanted a puppy, I got her a rescue dog. She didn't care about her birthday, I gave her a surprise party. She had never left the States, I took her on two all-expense-paid vacations, first-class seats. The perks were endless. For years, she never picked up a dinner check if I was there, when we were having a girls' day out. I gladly paid for any weekend excursions until I didn't.

There isn't a big mystery that it is easier to be and feel used by those closest to us. And we take for granted the ones who always show up for us. From a practical standpoint, most people will seek assistance from people in their immediate circle. If you break the ties that bind you, if you bite the hand that feeds you, why would you then direct your anger toward the person who has shown you a long history of good deeds?

Back then, I was dim-witted like an adjustable light bulb turned low. I didn't expect to receive on the level in which I had given because I was in a position where I had more than some. I was looking for a fair—not equal—exchange. I was looking for reciprocity, and continually, I was let down. There are so many ways to show up for someone if you don't have money. You have time, or advice, or a sympathetic ear.

If Blair liked to give Facebook shout-outs—why was I excluded? And if Blair bought thank you T-shirts—why was I not included? Instead, my kindness was received and discarded and somehow this person who showed up for all the freebies walked away as if she was a victim. Even though Blair doesn't acknowledge the good deeds, it doesn't erase that she received them. If she can't understand why she wasn't taken on that trip, then she doesn't understand systems. If something (person, organization, company, or nature) keeps providing and there is no return on their investment, the giving will stop. Everything functions through reciprocity. You can't have a car for transportation and not gas it up. Reciprocity—one of the easiest mathematical equations ever!

For me, I couldn't sit around getting fat off steak, while folks dined on sardines, so I shared. I didn't equally divide my income amongst the fray, but I tried to give those I loved the things they longed for if I could. I gave in moderation. I now understand that the resentment did not come because I didn't give, it came because I didn't give *it all*.

I was locked into altruistic behavior for years. That was my love language. I was a sympathizer, and it left me open to manipulation.

Blair's sharp tongue helped me identify my weaknesses. She was correct. I was a people-pleaser. I loved seeing people happy, and if I could play a small role in that, then I would.

Then I had to examine her comment about buying love. Was that my motivator? Did I have to purchase the love of family? I had to still my mind and meditate on that. The "why" kept bugging me. Why at eighteen with barely two nickels to rub together was I sponsoring kids in Africa after watching an infomercial? Why?

Studies have shown that the brains of people who engage in altruistic behavior are stimulated in pleasurable ways, similar to having sex or eating chocolate. People who partake in selfless acts and charitable work apparently see benefits. Darwin said that altruism is "an essential part of the social instincts." So whether my acts were saintly or I was unabashedly exploiting those less fortunate, my past efforts were now stunted.

So there I was in another transitional period in my life. I didn't know this, but all these lessons were arrows pointing right toward *cheap*. If I gave what I wanted when I wanted, the benefactor would find fault with me. If I gave what they wanted, when they wanted it, the benefactor would have control over me. I had to resist my urge to act out of kindness. So how do I quench my charitable thirst? Well, I shifted my focus to charities. That way I could give in anonymity without being judged, ridiculed, or made to feel as though my efforts were inadequate.

Pointedly, I could name countless situations where good deeds went awry. I could name several people with similar stories of altruism that did not end well. I'm sure you have your stories too. As I thought broadly about my selfless acts, those close to home, and also by volunteering, admittedly there were far more good deeds that did not go amiss. Still, I remain ambivalent regarding the risks vs. reward of doing good deeds for family and friends alike.

Altruistic Pros:

◊ **Good Deeds** could help with your health. Blair helped me realize that I was gaining something. Doing good deeds made me feel good. Endorphins were being released, and I felt naturally happy seeing someone else happy.

◊ **Good Deeds** may give you a needed break from your reality. Pouring into someone's life, carrying their burden, helped distract me from mine.

◊ **Good Deeds** should prompt you to stop and give thanks for your blessings. Helping someone who had an unexpected tragedy would force me to still my mind and appreciate not only that I was in a place where I could assist, but also center me to be grateful for the position I was in.

Altruistic Cons:

◊ **Road To Hell:** What if you have time management issues? Now you're saddled with additional distractions, and you place a person's need before your own.

◊ **Road To Hell:** You can do only so much for so many! Depending on the situation, if it's too large a deed and you take it on anyway, you could begin to feel fatigued. Have you heard, "she bit off more than she could chew?"

◊ **Road To Hell:** Should you take on a person's situation, you have stepped into the shoes of the problem solver. When problems don't get solved then the blame game comes into play.

◊ **Road To Hell:** Money issues. If your good deeds consistently involve the outlay of money; if your charitable acts aren't a diversified portfolio of cash and cashless acts of kindness, then it is time to rebalance.

Wherever you fall under the good deed/road to hell umbrella, place a cap on charity. Remember your budget or the 50/20/30 rule? Do not permit your good deeds to place you in debt or hinder you from climbing out of it. Should you allow your altruism to spill into other areas, such as savings, have a number on what you can afford to sacrifice. A good deed could be a loan. But what if that loan is never repaid? Many people say I don't lend money; I gift it because I know I won't get it back. Have a number on what you can afford to lose.

Remember what Darwin argued and what neuroscientists have proven. There is altruism in most everyone. It's never easy saying no. However, at some point you need to reach your quota on good deeds. If you came to that same person with the same situation after you helped them and was told no, would you get upset? Would it ruin the friendship? Could you live with it?

If you still have an altruistic itch that you need to scratch, here are other fulfilling ways to be charitable.

Ways Of Being Charitable:

◊ Volunteer your time at food banks or local pantries. Take it a step further by collecting canned food donations from your friends and neighbors.

◊ Help your local church by volunteering to be an usher, meet and greet, clean up, and organize.

◊ Habitat for Humanity is an amazing organization that gives back to many communities.

◊ Check out your local animal shelter and ask them if they're looking for volunteers. These shelters are incredibly invaluable and usually underfunded, and they can always use someone to help bathe and groom the animals, clean out cages, and take dogs on walks.

◊ Tithes. You can support the church you are a member of, but if you find yourself listening to podcasts of pastors of mega churches, make a donation. Just remember to budget.

◊ Non-profit organizations are a good way to give back. A favorite of mine is St. Jude[6].

◊ Pay it forward. A way I get my good deed fix is when I am on a flight, I will comp the person sitting next to me. Each year I have an airline credit of $200 and incentive from one of my credit cards that I pay in full each month. Depending on how often I fly that year, I usually only use a fraction of it. So on flights, I'm sort of Ms. Claus—You want another Heineken? It's on me! But remember to pay it forward! Two bucks for those headphones? No problem! Don't forget, pay it forward. The spontaneous good deeds are ALWAYS appreciated. And most importantly, it does not cost me one dime AND it makes me feel good.

🕑 Meditative Minutes

Meditate on why you do, don't, or have stopped doing good deeds. And once you find the answer, see if you want to continue, change, or reevaluate your position.

---

6   I am not a paid sponsor of St. Jude, nor am I endorsing this organization for financial gain. I, personally, like what they stand for. Donating is a personal choice of mine.

Cheap Girls Club Oath

You should have realized by now as you're reading this book that I had penny-wise and pound-foolish moments. If words like, dumb ass, moron, and stupid come to mind, good! I've evoked an emotion from you, which means that I've done my job (at my expense). My grandmother told me years ago that if an actor gets me to love or despise a character then they're a good actor.

Here's an exercise I want you to do.

Let's just say that we tallied up all the misspending I've done throughout the years and it totaled $500 (yeah, right) and had placed that sum into, let's keep it American, Coca Cola stock. Let's date it back to pre-911, because post 911 new investors were afraid to invest. Do you know that had you dumped $500 in 1986 to 2016 that same sum of money (no additions) would be $23,202? Don't believe me? Do it for yourself.

Visit: https://www.portfoliovisualizer.com/backtest-portfolio, add the stock's ticker symbol, KO and boom, in black and white.

I can't stress this enough! Be CHEAP with your money! Now if that doesn't make you look at ingrates through a different lens, then I don't know what will.

Maybe you see yourself as the ungrateful receiver but don't have to courage to admit that this is who you are. Or before reading this you never thought there was anything wrong always being the one on the receiving end. You have to make gratitude a practice with your children (should you have any) and in your life. Don't take a person's financial sacrifice for granted.

Chapter Fifteen

Spending Triggers

Most of us can say we are guilty of at least one spending spree, some of us can admit to more. Buying things you cannot afford, depleting your savings, and living on credit until that runs out can be taxing on your mental and physical health. Once you're in too deep, you often wonder: (a) How did I get here? and (b) How can I police myself to not go there again? This chapter isn't about budgeting to pay back what you've spent; it's about pinpointing what causes the problem and then finding a workable solution.

So, my dearest Cheap Girls, how can we stop spending if we don't recognize our triggers? Let's identify what prompts us to crack open our wallets, whip out those credit and debit cards, and drop serious cash on nonessentials. If shopping has become your favorite pastime, and your answer to what you do for fun, then you must get your spending under control before your finances implode.

Spending triggers are symptoms of an underlying cause. Sever the root. Kill the problem. Russian psychologist Ivan Pavlov studied conditioning when he took first notice that even when he wasn't bringing his dogs food, they would salivate when he walked in the room. This behavior was unconditioned. He then rang a bell when he brought the food, and the dogs would salivate. After several experiments, Pavlov rang the bell without the food—which is conditioning—and the dogs salivated. The controlled, conditioned stimulus leads to a controlled, conditioned response. Pavlov's experiment proves that we can change our behavior with training.

When family, friends, and associates are competing with you, and you do not understand that you're in a competition, conversations become awkward. The show-and-tell climate becomes like a pressure cooker, and if you don't recognize that it's a trigger, you could go on a spending spree to prove something to someone who will never see you other than as they want. Don't be a racehorse jockeying for first place on someone's timeline. Their perceptions and misconceptions of you should have no value in your life. You may lose friends, you may lose family, but don't leverage those relationships at the costs of your savings, financial freedom, and retirement. Seek, know, and realize those outside influences are triggers.

Erin, a friend of mine, keeps measuring her quality of life and happiness on whether she can outspend me. Her endorphins are only elevated if she feels as if she's the talk of the town. Once I knew that her satisfaction was based on whether she could one-up me, I knew I could control her. For instance, if I bought a stock, and then years later Erin bought that same stock, she would obsessively call to find out how many shares I purchased. Repeatedly she would ask, "So how many shares you got?" And consistently, I would be evasive. Each phone call she would hang up frustrated, until she thought that my life was a "Bow Wow challenge." Her opinions were of no consequence. I was already on my journey and would allow no one to veer me off course. Her unconditioned trigger was kicked into gear when Erin sought a controlled competition. Her obsession to compare apples, to control and magnify her image, is all rooted in arrested development. When your purchases are predicated on upstaging someone, and the only purpose of asking probative questions is to feel a false sense of superiority, then that's a spending trigger.

This revelation is new. I am a few years evolved, and now I'm amazed when someone pops their head up and tries to drag me into a spending competition. I pay 100% of my overhead; no one is splitting my costs, no parent with fixed income is contributing to the household, and there's no trust fund I could dip into. The only person who has to repay your debt is you. Remember that if you find yourself allowing outside influences, public opinions, or agitators to sow into your life.

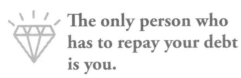

The only person who has to repay your debt is you.

We all have obstacles, some more than others. If you feel that you've chosen the short stick, as my nine-year-old niece told me one day, deal with it. I was wallowing in self-pity, going on and on about some thing or another, and she walked over to me with a meme on her smartphone that read: Deal with it. Don't avoid it, and don't spend money to mask it. Occasionally, we can all get down and feel sorry for ourselves, but spending is the cause, not the remedy. Learn to handle obstacles, because they come to everyone trying to do something great. So, yeah, deal with it.

What's your stimulus? What triggers your spending? You must figure out the association between emotional stressors and shopping. Find the catalyst that pushes you into your spending routine.

Spending Triggers

Stress

Stress is a big spending trigger. Physiological and psychological stressors from work and home life can do a number on your financial bottom line. Spending to relieve stress can have an opposite result. Triggers are sometimes prompted by stress. Stress eating, stress shopping, stress sexting—stress precipitates the action, and instant gratification momentarily quiets the hunger before you have to repeat the behavior.

Good news

You get great news, and you want to reward yourself, so you splurge on a big-ticket item or several smaller purchases. This becomes habit-forming. Each time something goes your way, you tell yourself that you deserve to be rewarded. If not monitored, good news turns into just "news," good or bad, and you rack up debt. Shopping to reward yourself, but are you?

Social media

Social media has become a never-ending reel of lifestyles of the rich and famous. The peer pressure of your high-school days has made its way back into your adult life. People spend to keep up or fit in, and the "likes" and "followers" becomes the vehicle that drives their overspending.

Holidays

Most of us love the holidays and emotionally spend on loved ones. If Christmas carols or July 4th shenanigans seduce you into breaking the bank each year, the holidays are your spending triggers.

People-pleasing

Many people will overspend to buy the love of others. You are looking for positive reinforcement from that person. As I have stated, I found that people-pleasing was one of my spending triggers. Unfortunately, I found I had more than one.

Shopping addiction

Retail therapy is so common, they gave it a cutesy name that justifies the spending. Had a bad day? No problem. Just have some "retail therapy," and things will be awesome sauce! If you get a shopper's high, look for the cause before the effect is debt. Retail therapy should never be a solution to any problem if it's frequently done. If it leads to debt, then a shopping addiction needs to be addressed.

Depression

Depression, either clinical or situational, is another trigger that could lead to debt. If a tragic event has befallen some people or they've sunken into a dark place, they use shopping as a quick relief from pain.

Credit cards

You get that new credit card or line of credit, and you think you're rich. Your fingers are itching to take that card out and break it in. Credit cards, in general, can trigger overspending because the shopper doesn't instantly feel the pinch at the point of purchase as they would with a cash sale.

Image

Usually, we don't see that some grooming habits are triggered when someone compliments our appearance. We girls spend an incredible amount of cash upholding our image on these self-esteem boosters:

nails, hair, makeup, eyebrow and bikini waxing, fillers, cosmetic surgery, tanning beds.

Subterfuge

Your spending trigger could come in a gift. Like the Trojan horse, you readily accept the free upgrade from an airline from coach to first class. You sit back in the comfy leather seat with the extra leg room, free drinks, and you're hooked. The introductory teaser to the good life is just the catalyst that makes you crave more. How can you ever go back to basic when you've experienced baller? Now all your flights must be first class. Why would you travel any other way?

Gambling

The dreamer, the person looking for a quick come-up, or the person with grandiose dreams could spend days gambling. Legal and illegal gambling quickly leads to debt.

Does any of this ring true? Whenever I needed a pick-me-up, I shopped. Shopping was an activity for me. As some would enjoy kickboxing or bowling, I found joy at the mall. Clothing was a visual stimulus that made me emotionally high. I would feel inebriated while shopping, and then once the credit card statements came, I would crash. After I had discovered my triggers, I placed myself on a spending diet and used preventative measures to recognize, avoid, and overcome my addiction. Below are some tools to assist you with overcoming your Achilles heel.

Solutions

Don't break the budget

A budget should always be in place for special occasions and holidays where overspending is standard practice.

Give it a minute

When you find yourself with extra cash, have no knee-jerk reaction to spending it all. Take time to cool off by walking away from the purchase. Should you come back later, ask yourself why do you need this, could you live without the item, and what do you hope to get from this item?

Fight temptation

Unsubscribe to any stores' e-mailing marketing lists. You don't want to be tempted by their advertising sorcery.

Reach out

If you find yourself depressed-shopping, pick up the phone and connect with family and friends.

Re-center

Should a stressful situation occur and you find yourself perusing your favorite retail websites or about to jump in your car to head to the mall, stop. Close your eyes and take deep breaths. Try to clear your mind and get centered.

Be yourself

How others think, feel, or see you is inconsequential. Should you find yourself trapped between ego and image and see no way out other than making a purchase, just note that if you submit, if you cave into the pressure, then you are allowing another person to have control over YOUR life. Your actions, your thoughts, and how you spend YOUR money are up to you.

Get off the one-sided see-saw

If you're tempted to pick up the tab, buy a gift for a person you care about, ask what has this person done for you lately, or ever? Odds are, if you are the people-pleaser, then that person is the receiver. Your answer will be a resounding nothing. So that's what you should do for that person. NOTHING.

 Meditative Minutes

Take a moment to meditate on the triggers that rang true for you. Which made you emotional or defensive?

 Cheap Girls Club Oath

You can't stop the leak if you don't find the source. Be brave and face your triggers with the fortitude of a Cheap Girl.

Chapter Sixteen

The Art of Saying No

The most powerful word you will ever speak is *no*. Here's the thing, though. Many of us cannot say it. You want to say it, but when you're asked point-blank for a favor you hedge, trip over your words, leave room for ambiguity, and finally, you concede. In hindsight you realize that *no* could have saved you from overextending yourself. You tell yourself that next time will be different—the next time someone comes to you for anything you will say *no*, but oddly enough, you can't.

When you're on the financial recovery road, you've created a budget, and you're paying down debt, people will come from all angles to disrupt your progress with their agendas. Why should you get out of debt when they're still in it? They'll ask for that loan from you so they can get on their feet, and if you can't say *no*, then you fell for it. I have worn that dunce hat until I thought it was a badge of honor. I felt honorable in helping others before myself. When I learned that you must build yourself up first, strengthen your weak limbs, thicken your roots, and flourish before you pour into someone else's life, I paused.

First, you have to allow your bank account to swell, burst at the seams, and overflow. If there's a little extra spilling out, then that's what you bless others with, but only if you want to. When you continue to put people needs ahead of your own, when you consistently place yourself last in your own life, you will suffer. The only ones you should have an obligation to are you and the children you bring into this world until the age of majority. Unless you want to do more. And you should stop wanting to do more if you're not in a strong financial position to do so.

Airlines have a policy; save yourself, first. When that oxygen mask drops, you are to first place it over your mouth and then help others. Instinctually, you may want to save your neighbor, child, or companion first—but you would do that to your own detriment, and there would be no way for you to help them. With finances, the same philosophy should apply.

Retrospectively, the moment I saw a financial increase, I was trying to save everyone. When I told those close to allow me to go ahead of them, build a strong foundation for myself, and then I would come back for them, I was met with judgment, resentment, and hostility. I was isolated and then cut off. That took years to process. The knowledge that takes time to materialize is called wisdom. I wanted to please, I wanted to be liked by everybody, but they didn't like me. They liked my favors, my money, and my willingness to be there when their dollars fell short.

People compartmentalize most things. Friends will place you in a category and keep you there. There's the jokester, an individual who lifts their spirits telling jokes and being silly. The drama queen, who is always over the top with it. The wise one, always spreading seeds of wisdom to those thirsty enough to drink it in. The volatile one, who erupts in anger over the most trivial things. These girls are entertainment. A comedy show, a violent show, a wise owl, a melodramatic act. They're the stimulus that most people instinctually keep around. And then there's the dependable person. You. You're not there to make them laugh, you will not have them under duress or afraid to go outside. You're the person they call upon when they want something. If they want you to be a good listener, you will give them your time. Pick up their children from school, you're Uber. When they need someone to feed their ego, you'll tell them that they're smart, beautiful, and kind. And when they need someone to loan them money, pick up the dinner tab, or treat them to pricey things, you're the sucker.

But now you're in the club. And time, experiences, and awareness have taught you that the road to hell is drenched with sweat, tears, and your goodwill. If you're still having trouble reconciling this, let's list the reasons people find it hard to say *no*.

Reasons we say yes:

◊ We don't want to lose a friendship.
◊ You may feel guilty if the friend in need loses what they were trying to keep by asking you for the loan.
◊ You don't want to seem like a selfish person.
◊ NO could lead to friends to gossip about you, and you don't want the negative attention.
◊ The stigma of being unkind or uncaring outweighs the favor.
◊ You think you might need them in the future. Yet, you don't realize that they will never be there for you in the same capacity as you were for them, if at all.

Write out a list of all the "yeses" you've obligated yourself to in the last year. Once you've listed them all out, ask yourself who benefited from the *yes* and if the reasons above are enough for justification. The list should read like this: FAVOR. RESULT. BENEFICIARY.

Here's what my list looked like:

Favor	Result	Beneficiary
Allowed a person to move into a rental property which would save her $1500/per month on lowered rent.	The friend ended up with a savings of $18,000 per year.	Allowing a friend the "friends and family" discounted rental rate did not earn me X amount of dollars each month she was there. Because if I didn't rent the property for its full market value, then I was losing money each month. So the person who benefited was the friend who netted an $18K savings per year, for five years.
Loaned a cousin a $1000 to pay his rent arrears.	He was never backed up on rent. He took the money and went shopping for Ralph Lauren shirts and designer jeans to impress some girl. He never repaid the loan.	I received nothing from this act. I did not feel good about. I did not want to do it. So, my cousin was the benefactor.
A friend asked me to write her autobiography in my "free" time.	The Cheap Girls Club movement had already begun. This favor I turned down.	Had I written this book, it would have been done as a favor, as she stressed that she had no money to pay for my ghost writing services. No one has 1000 hours of "free" time to give away, but, that's what she kept asking of me. The only one who would have benefited would have been her. I turned her down. I lost nothing. She gained nothing.

Now, what does your list look like? Be honest about why you say *yes*. Why are you agreeing to things to your detriment? Tell yourself the absolute truth and listen to your answer because it might surprise you.

Here are some things to say *no* to. Post it on your refrigerator.

Just Say No List:

Loans

We've already established why it is never good to make personal loans. Not only is there no guarantee that you'll be repaid, but the borrower almost always has an attitude with you when repayment is due. Save yourself from a headache and say NO.

Weddings

Girls always love when we're asked to be in a wedding party. We feel as though we won something if we're picked. And then you must deal with Bridezilla who wants a marriage equivalent to Princess Di. Your dress and shoes cost a fortune, as does your hair, makeup, bridal shower, bachelorette party, gifts and a host of expenses, but the bride has a snobby attitude. Trust me, say NO. Politely decline, but go to the wedding and budget for a lovely gift. You will save yourself a world of a headache and debt.

Godparent

If you don't have children then you may be the first person a mom asks to be their child's godparent. If your finances are in order, then you will definitely be asked. That title has been watered down and diluted to only mean you send gifts throughout the year and help contribute to the child's education. You are not really there to raise the child as your own should some tragedy befall the parents. Why would they choose you and you're in the nightclub every night? And, rightfully so; you have no children. Why would they choose you when they have family and grandparents, and so on and so forth? Say, NO. Another thing to note, you have no rights to that child. Should the mother suddenly decide that you are no longer welcome in their lives because you two had some arbitrary argument, you can't go petition the court to ask for visitation. It's over. You're done. And whatever you've done for that child, treating her/him as if they were your own—get this through your head—they're not.

Kid Parties

If you don't have children stay away from their parties. I know most kid parties are really for the adults, so you may think there's no harm in going. The booze, the food, is all for those 21 and over. But have you ever stopped to reflect on how much of a drain these parties are on your finances? When you don't have children, people expect you to bring the good gifts. Why? Because you're childless so you should have lots of cash. The parents start in on you early. "Oh, little Isabella is doing so well in school. She needs an iPad, though, to keep up with her studies. Come here, Bella, and give Auntie a hug." (And you're not her aunt.) The only girls that should attend a child's party are mothers. That way, there's reciprocity. You buy my kid a hat, I will buy your child gloves. Get it? Great.

Favors

Again, keep favors in the NO column. The help-me-move-into-my-new-place and could-you-drop-my-car-off-to-get-serviced favors should no longer be considered.

Credit

You already know the right thing to say, and the right thing to do. Do not sign or cosign for anyone on a loan. I have my opinion about mingling finances with the hubby too, but that's another book.

Houseguest

You have a longtime friend who suddenly finds herself homeless and she wants to stay with you for just a couple weeks until she gets settled. Say NO. However she found herself in that situation allow her to find her way out. Or let her family carry her burden. But if you value the friendship, saying NO will ensure that it remains. Sure, she'll be upset at first, but you will still have a friend. If you give in and allow her to come in and mooch off you, turn your household upside down, then you'll have regrets.

Time

Be cheap with your time. Time is something that we can't actually make up for. We can say in theory that we are making up for lost time, but that's a misnomer. Stop allowing people to usurp your time, calling you with gossip, negativity, or begging for favors. Social media too is a significant drain on your day. Unless you're promoting your business, scrolling through timelines, posting pictures, and uploading videos are all time-consuming and have zero ROI. Say NO to allowing outside influences to monopolize your time.

Advice

Be cheap when doling out advice. When a person is in a dilemma they can't solve and they come to you frightened and teary-eyed, mind your business. Say, "No, sorry, I can't help on this one." Because should they take your advice on a matter they know is a losing situation, the moment all hell breaks loose it will be your fault, not theirs, for creating the mess.

And while we're on the subject, be leery of the advice you receive. Don't take business advice from someone who's never run a company. Don't look to single friends to give advice on your marriage. And don't ever take money advice from someone who is not on your financial level or above. Why? Most times, wanting to see your downfall, their advice will always be the opposite of what you should do. If you hear, "That's what I would do," run.

Work Related

Keep your distance from any work-related activities and unnecessary socializing. The one thing I will never miss is office politics. You're forced to socialize, contribute, and do it all with a smile. It feels like every week an envelope would be passed around for someone you never met or hardly know. "Sally up in Finance is retiring. We all need to contribute ten bucks toward that." And "Joan has started selling Mary Kay for extra income. We should all purchase a lip gloss to show her our support." How many birthdays and promotions have you contributed to when you didn't want to? Whatever you do, don't reach in your wallet because it will never end. Say NO.

Girl Scout Cookies

This one vexes me a lot. Is it because those darn cookies are so expensive, or is it because I am still traumatized that I never received my 200 bucks worth? Cross my heart, I didn't. I coughed up two hundred bucks to help out a mom with a sob story about her child never outselling anyone, and I waited. And waited. I called repeatedly, and it was always, "Next week I'll send them to you." Nevertheless, parents passing those order forms around, hovering, are annoying. So, NO, nobody wants your evil cookies.

It's usually the same person or persons always looking for someone else to problem-solve. And *yes* was an introduction to a lifetime of putting their needs before your own. I've heard advice that you should tell a person to let you pray on it before you decide whether you will help. Or give you time to think it over before you decide on whether or not to support. I say, freak all that. Just say no. Your third eye, intuition, or spirit already warned you that you should say *no*. Taking time to pray or ruminate over the problem is just prolonging the inevitable and leaving room for you to waver. Say it quick, without hesitation, and be done with it. It should always be about what you want. This is your life, and no one should have ownership over it. Being backed into imaginary corners, bamboozled, or bullied into the yes zone should be no more.

If you think about all the times you said *yes* to someone, how many of those times was it authentic, something you really wanted to say *yes* to? Most likely, you said *yes* for all the wrong reasons, none of which was helping you live your most authentic life. How uncomfortable is it when people come to you for favors you don't want to do? In a perfect world, we could help everyone without overextending ourselves. We could over-commit, overpromise, and overachieve without losing an ounce of sleep.

Be cheap with you! Say NO more.

For me, so many had cast their issues upon my shoulders that even if I mustered the strength to say no, the lingering feeling of resentment took up residence in my head. My mind would be cluttered with the remnants of guilt. Why can't I help them out? Or what can I do to help them out? I would be up all night trying to fix someone else's problem, and in the morning they would ask me what *our* solution was. Being boggled down with someone else's problem is not a way to live. Most of us have limited resources, limited energy, and limited money, yet we consistently deplete our reserves for others.

You must let people go. Once you know how you fit into someone's life, if that placemat isn't mutually beneficial, if there isn't reciprocity, let her go! Let them go, him go, the dog, cat—whatever isn't bringing joy or constructively contributing in your life must go. Be cheap with you! Say NO more.

So you ask, What's the art of saying no? It's to just say it. Say, NO! If you thought I would have deep, meaningful, Oprah-esque, "Let me pray about it," type of advice, sorry. I tried that method, and it just doesn't work. They will use their God against your God. You're like, "I prayed on it, and God told me I shouldn't do it." And their reply will be, "God said to me you should!"

 Meditative Minutes

When succinctly stated, NO as an instrument can block you from being used and exploited into doing things you do not want to do for people you don't want to help. Sometimes it's good to unplug, take yourself off the grid, and meditate not on having the strength to say *no*, but being OK with saying it.

Cheap Girls Club Oath

Don't overanalyze and don't apologize, because it gives room for the person to get inside your head and have you second-guessing why you placed yourself before them. Soon, no will get easier. It will instinctively roll off your tongue, and you'll leave the problem with its original owner. Don't end up on *Judge Judy* suing for gas money. The only large sum of money I will give out will be an inheritance. Yes, I must die first. Promise yourself that you'll take the oath of NO!

Chapter Seventeen

Be the Treasurer of Your Life

omen. We give life, we give love. We are givers by nature. And what do we receive? On a national average, we receive .79 cents on the dollar our male counterparts earn. If you are a woman of color, the wage gap is substantially higher. An African American female will earn 65% of a white male; Hispanic women, 55%. If those numbers aren't disturbing to you, they should be. They should be enough for you to look at money differently.

In 2015, Academy Award-winning actor Jennifer Lawrence went on record to bring awareness to the gender wage gap in Hollywood after a Sony hack revealed that Lawrence and Amy Adams were allegedly paid a fraction of what the male costars were paid for the movie *American Hustle*. Soon the topic trended, and many Hollywood notables such as Amy Adams, Robin Wright, and Patricia Arquette joined the discussion. Hollywood, the billionaire boys club, responded by saying that the male actors all negotiated higher wages, pointing out that the women could have done the same. Lawrence remarks she didn't fight for more because she feared not being liked, or called a brat, or branded as *difficult*, a constant worry for women.

Several studies have shown that women who ask for promotions or raises have been the target of subsequent bullying, are ostracized, or face dire consequences and realize that the risk is too big. The whole ordeal makes them feel uncomfortable, and the stigma of being labeled difficult is tough to endure. While Lawrence can complain and write an op-ed piece about receiving $17 million as opposed to $25 million, a woman of color would be given a lot less for the same role in the same movie.

Google is another powerhouse being sued in a class action suit for allegedly participating in pay discrimination against women. It has long been rumored that technology companies do not promote women to leadership positions and pay female techs less than male techs for similar jobs.

The revolution has been televised, and yet the scales of justice still lean toward men. Statistically, a woman will earn slightly over ten thousand dollars less per year than a man—same work, same hours. Imagine, if at the end of each year you received an additional $10,000 bonus. What would you do with that money? Well, men, they would invest it. Ask yourself this: How many female billionaires are there? How many high-ranking bankers are women? Men dive into the numbers game early. And let's not discuss the cost of being a woman or the politics of our healthcare and right to choose. It's time for financial empowerment. Beyoncé said it best—Girls run the world. But, first, we must balance our checkbooks.

Universally, we should be the CFOs of our lives. Before I fully understood a Ponzi scheme, I knew the risk of what's called a sou-sou. A sou-sou, known by different names in other countries, is a familiar concept worldwide. It is generally but not exclusively practiced in the workplace, where members join the savings or loan club. Each member pays a specific set amount of capital, usually collected per pay period. The treasurer holds all the money and each month disperses the pot to one member, which is the full amount collected that month. Let's say you have 12 members who contribute $800 per person, per month to the pot, each member will receive $9,600 until the sou-sou is dissolved. So if you are the first member to receive your sou-sou—the full $9600—you still have an obligation (loan repayment) to contribute the twelve payments of $800 until each member has been paid.

This system heavily relies on trust. You have to trust the treasurer to keep that amount of funds in a safe place, you have to believe that the other members will continue to contribute to the pot after they've received their sou-sou, and you have to trust that no unforeseen circumstances arise. There are just too many unpredictable variables for me to cosign on this system. Take note that there aren't legal agreements signed when you're handing over your money. There aren't any promissory notes, there aren't even any handshakes. It is, literally, whoever wants in is in.

I can, however, understand the allure of it all if you're first up. Even members two through five on the list could make an argument on why this non-FDIC loan is smart. But any slot after that, to me, is just dumb. The silliest person on the list of members is the member who clocks in at number twelve. To have a stranger, coworker, friend, family member hold your money for twelve months, interest-free, in a shoebox in their closet is asinine. You are gambling on the good will, morals, and ethics of another. I find this system to be antiquated and reminiscent of when your ancestors hid their money in a cereal box in the pantry or under their mattresses. As you can surmise, from being burned numerous times, my trust in humans is slim. Investing in a sou-sou is high-risk behavior.

I began with the sou-sou scenario because I had a friend who approached me with what is called a pyramid scheme, and my sou-sou distrust came in handy. The word "pyramid" was never spoken in her sales pitch. Around this time I had been doing research to open a brokerage account. I had my eyes on Rite Aid stock. Why Rite Aid? I liked all the new buildings that were being built around neighborhoods. The buildings were aesthetically pleasing. That was it. The money I had saved was burning a hole in my pockets, and I was eager to invest it in something and watch it grow.

My friend had a good job, and her base salary was triple what I was making. I respected her work ethic—she was one hard-working woman—but I didn't respect her morals. When she came to me with a "business" proposition, there was a powerful feeling of betrayal coursing through my veins. She explained that she was working part-time with this new company, and that if I invested $5000 with her, I could make $50,000 in less than two weeks. She was talking big money!

I pressed for details, just to see her fumble over her words, lose direct eye contact with me, and begin to shift her weight from one leg to the next. I asked where was the $50,000 going to come from, and she said that I had to find other investors.

"And then what?"

"I don't understand," she replied.

"What are we investing in?"

"You're the boss. You find the people to invest in you, and then they find people to invest under them."

"So there's no product. We're not selling anything or investing into something? No stock?"

"I'm telling you it's a company. I'll get you the name of it later. I was brought in by this lady. She's made over a hundred thousand. She brought me in, and I'm bringing you in."

"So this is a pyramid scheme?"

"Noooo!" she screamed. "It is not!"

"Is it a sou-sou?"

"It's business."

Whatever she called it, it was all semantics. The fact was that it was illegal. What I knew then was that ascension takes time. Anytime someone is offering 500% return on your investment in two weeks, run. You have to leave friendship on the floor when it comes to your finances. You have to think, and live cheap. Whatever sounds too good to be true is. Not "usually" is or "maybe" is—it unequivocally is a farce. And the easiest victims to get scammed are those closest to the con artist. Con artists prey upon family and friends because they ask the least amount of questions and the trust is built-in. They don't have to earn it.

Leave your friendship on the floor when it comes to your finances.

The Bernie Madoff scandal reverberated throughout the world. This was the largest Ponzi scheme scandal in history, clocking in at 65 billion. Notwithstanding the cautionary tale aspect of it, fundamentally, greed is at the core. And a greedy person is just as dangerous as a loaded gun. They will keep firing until, eventually, they hit someone. The sobering truth is, there wasn't any way to forecast that an investment firm in good standing would flip, mid-operation, to a Ponzi.

To be the treasurer of your life means that perhaps you don't place all your eggs in one basket. The people most affected by Madoff, the ones who couldn't bounce back from the scandal, are the people who invested their entire retirement with a single firm. When you hear diversify, your ears should perk up and you should take heed. I have tremendous empathy for these victims because, pre-Madoff scandal, I would have dumped 100% of my retirement with someone as respected and renowned as Bernie. However the lesson starts somewhere, and it usually starts with a victim. You only know the pot is hot because of the poor fool who touched it.

Life is full of lessons, ones you learn and ones you earn. If everyone could see 100 miles down the road, how well off would we be? If overnight wealth is your destination, then you will be more susceptible to making bad financial investments on your journey. A sou-sou isn't illegal, but the uncertainty of it, being non-FDIC insured, raises a red flag for me personally. A pyramid scheme relies on earning money through participants, while a Ponzi scheme is based on making money through investments—these both are illegal and depend on trusting victims.

So how can we be the treasurer of our lives? Well, it starts with financial awareness.

Stay Woke

◊ Check your monthly statements (bank, credit cards, and investments) for accuracy. Nowadays with financial institutions you can monitor your accounts for accuracy instantaneously should you connect your accounts to your smartphone. Alternatively, you can sign in once a week from your desktop.

◊ Create long (sixteen characters or more), complex passwords mixing numbers, letters, and symbols and replace with a new one quarterly.

◊ For increased security, sign up for alerts (text[7]/e-mail). Most bank and credit cards offer alerts where you are in control. You set spending and transaction alerts where you are notified in real time if the minimum

---

7   Check your mobile plan. Additional rates could apply.

posted item exceeds your specified limit or if any of your profile information has been updated (passwords, addresses, etc). You can receive a text, e-mail, or both, whenever movement is on your accounts.

◊ If offered, always sign up for two-step authentication. This requires a free app, like Google Authenticator, or a code sent to your phone or e-mail before access to the account is granted.

◊ You should always have virus protection, especially with sensitive information. As a precautionary measure, do not save any financial documents to your hard drive. Hackers could get a wealth of privileged information. Use external hard drives for sensitive data.

◊ Another bad practice is having your personal information (date of birth, mother's maiden name, address, cell phone, high school and college) listed on your social media sites. Hackers can gather your sensitive data and use it to gain access to your accounts.

◊ All mail, junk mail, and discarded documents with personal and financial information should be shredded.

Almost any institution is susceptible to security breaches. Target, Home Depot, Anthem, and Equifax—just to name a few. To be the treasurer of your life, you have to proactively protect your identity.

In the past, I was skeptical about identity theft monitoring companies. I had my social security number so tightly shut down that I had issues opening up new credit lines. However, thieves keep evolving. When national news reported that identities are being sold for bitcoins and I didn't know what a bitcoin was, perhaps the extra monitoring could be something to consider. Below are a few options:

◊ Lifelock.com

◊ Identityforce.com

◊ Creditsesame.com

Here are additional ways to help you monitor and secure your credit history. Things a treasurer should do.

Security Freeze

A security freeze is a good idea to help delay you from applying for and receiving instant lines of new credit. If a lender can't access your reports, you should be denied. You can lift the credit freeze; however, before you do, you should take the time to consider if the purchase is wise. With data breaches and identity theft, a freeze could also minimize your risk of falling victim and limit your anxiety of someone wreaking havoc on your excellent credit rating and personal finances.

To add or lift a security freeze here are the three major credit bureaus. You can apply online, or download and print the applications and mail the documentation to each address. Some states offer this service for free. Other states charge a nominal fee.

◊ **Equifax Security Freeze**
   P.O. Box 105788
   Atlanta, Georgia 30348
   1-800-685-1111 (NY residents 1-800-349-9960)
   https://www.freeze.equifax.com/Freeze/jsp/SFF_PersonalIDInfo.jsp

◊ **Experian Security Freeze**
   P.O. Box 9554
   Allen, TX 75013
   1-888-397-3742
   https://www.experian.com/freez/center.html

◊ **TransUnion LLC**
   P.O. Box 2000
   Chester, PA 19022-2000
   1-888-909-8872
   https://www.transunion.com/credit-freeze/place-credit-freeze

Fraud Alert

In conjunction, think about adding a fraud alert to your account. The initial alert is for 90 days. Contact one of the three above credit bureaus to place the fraud alert on your credit report. Any bureau must communicate with the remaining two. For additional protection, think about an extended fraud alert, which lasts for seven years. You must submit a theft report with other verifiable information and mail your application to any of the three credit bureaus, who will contact the remaining companies. The reason I am stressing credit protection is because good credit history and rating does to your finances what eating right and exercising does for your body. Should you not be able to prove identity theft or fraud, you would be on the hook for a considerable amount of money. Restoring stolen funds, your reputation, and credit rating could cost you. Here are a couple considerations for credit monitoring, free and paid subscriptions.

Free Credit Monitoring:

◊ Creditkarma.com
◊ Creditsesame.com

Paid Credit Monitoring:

◊ Lifelock.com
◊ Truecredit.com

Credit History

Three Leading Credit Bureaus:

◊   Equifax - www.equifax.com.
    P.O. Box 740241. Atlanta, GA 30374-0241. 1-800-685-1111.

◊ Experian - www.experian.com.
P.O. Box 2104. Allen, TX 75013-0949. 1-888-EXPERIAN (397-3742).

◊ TransUnion - www.transunion.com. P.O. Box 1000. Chester, PA 19022. 1-800-916-8800.

Free Credit Reports:

You have the right to obtain a free copy of your credit report from all three reporting agencies every twelve months. Call the telephone numbers above and listen to the prompts. Keep in mind that nowadays, with identity theft, it would be wiser to do monthly credit checks. Some companies offer free monthly credit reports and updates, and some of these free offers include your FICO score.

◊ Experian.com.

◊ Freecreditreport.com

◊ Creditkarma.com – has two major reporting bureaus, TransUnion and Equifax.

◊ Creditcards.chase.com/free-credit-score?CELL=68GP

Credit Reports and FICO Score

Credit reports show your overall history (payment, revolving credit accounts, addresses, real estate, and installment payments), hard inquiries (credit checks by lenders or landlords), and potentially harmful information like late payments, loan defaults, collections, charge-offs, and public records.

Your **FICO credit score** is comprised of the data retrieved from the three major credit bureaus. Scores usually scale from 300-850. The higher the number, the higher your credit rating. Your score is the median number of the three agencies, Experian, Equifax, and TransUnion, and primarily forecasts your ability to pay back debt.

Generally, if your FICO score is 700 and above, you have Tier 1 or A type credit, which is the highest credit ranking. With this credit score, you usually qualify for lower annual percentage rates, which essentially saves you money on loans, something we cheap girls love.

In All Fairness

Singer Erykah Badu made the name Tyrone famous when she crooned about a deadbeat. This is me adding my two cents to situations that I see growing amongst our independent women. Should you find yourself with a live-in boyfriend, I hope you are not splitting the bills 50/50.

Ouch. I can hear the feminists cursing my name. But hear me out. Men should readily accept a higher percentage of the overhead as providers, and that doesn't diminish our independence. I've been a strong, independent person all my life. I was an emancipated child by age twelve and won't readily allow a man to carry my groceries. So I get it. If you're happy with those margins, don't allow my meddling to muck up a good thing.

This is a personal choice, however, I felt this was important enough to state. Even if the adjustment to the percentage is small, you two should discuss a 55/45 split on the bills. Think about it. Statistics don't lie. Men make more money than us doing the same job without justification. Now factor in the expenses involved with just maintaining our gender. "But what if we make the same amount of money?" you ask. Well, I still stand firmly on 55/45 (or some variation, as long as you get the favorable end of it). Alternatively, if you make a lot more, then 50/50 is just fine by me. Look, no one is going to protect you more than you. We're in our third millennium, and women are still getting the short end of the stick with no relief for our generation.

I have friends, this couple. The female's income is 2/3 less than her boyfriend. Do you think that's any concern of his? Not even remotely. They split all bills 50/50, and I watch as she does all the heavy lifting. She does the grocery shopping, cooking, all the cleaning, while he takes care of the joint finances, takes out the garbage, and should something break around the house, I guess he would fix it if he could. If not, they hire a professional, and she would pay half of that bill. He's self-employed, and she works in a field that puts a lot of stress on her body. He gets on my nerves as he walks through their apartment as if it's his castle. Everything is singular, "*My* this and *my* that."

One day while he was out, she was in tears. She was coming into some money, and he wanted to control it. He wanted to make a purchase for the house that she did not want to make because it would take all of her new money. The money for her would be her emergency fund, should the relationship not last. Ultimately, he got what he wanted. He had full control over her and her finances.

There are also girls out there who don't receive help toward rent and bills at all. Yes, you have the man, but not much else. To be the treasurer of your life, you cannot find yourself in these situations. Ever.

Wrap-Up

So the rundown should look like this:

- ◊ You should ask for a raise if you think that your work warrants one.
- ◊ Keep a close eye on your financial statements.
- ◊ Don't allow yourself to pay 50% of the household bills while doing 90% of the household chores.

To be the treasurer of your life, the house always wins. Make sure you're the house.

 ## Meditative Minutes

Meditate on the empowerment being your own treasurer will bring, and listen for the warning signals you may be consciously avoiding.

 ## Cheap Girls Club Oath

Ridiculous rates of return are as deceitful as the piper who played his flute to lure children to their deaths. Take an oath to vet all offers, investments, and deals that seem legit and too good to be true.

Chapter Eighteen

Decide How You Want to Live

You've learned ways to budget, save more, say no, and are on the road to spending less. Now you should decide on how you want to live. Imagine taking a wet towel and squeezing every drop of water out of it—that's what you should be doing with life. Live abundantly with purpose, deliberate intent, and mental clarity. Look for enlightenment in routines, and visualize your best life now. I chose a debt-free future. Paying creditors, dodging collection agents, and spending countless hours working overtime isn't my kind of nirvana. You deserve more. Now, believe that to be true, and so it shall.

The power of positivity is the secret sauce catching momentum for some time now. It's because people see real results with this practice. You have been blessed with this life, so decide how you want to live it. Focus on what you can control—saving, spending, and how you want your retirement to look. And accept the things you cannot. Optimism goes a long way for winners. If you always expect positive results, your journey could be transformative.

 Focus on what you can control. Accept what you cannot.

Cheap Girls Club Guide to Positivity

1. **See It:** Have a vision. And then create a vision board, if you have not already done so. All it takes is a flat surface (cardboard, cork board) and cut and paste what you want to attract. You can also use Pinterest to create a digital vision board. Be specific about what you want, and hone in on the emotions attached to each picture. How will you feel when this materializes? This works, but try not to be creepy about it. The hot, married, fitness trainer should not appear on your board.

2. **Speak It:** As often as you want, talk to others about how you see yourself and your life unfolding. Your goals, ambitions, and expectations should be put out into the universe. Prophesy your future and watch it flourish.

3. **Think It:** Meditation tips the scales. Center your thoughts to channel only positivity and bask in all good things to come. Start with just ten minutes a day, and watch how things change.

4. **Watch It** materialize.

If you want to live a debt-free life, you must make it a priority. I did. It doesn't happen accidentally. There has to be structured, focused intent. Be clear about your choices. The great thing about taking a proactive approach to living an awesome, financially free life is the empowerment that comes with it. The copious amounts of money, time, and energy that went into creating (and avoiding) the debt will no longer be. Arguments with the hubby over finances? Gone. Dodging creditors and collection calls? Gone. Late nights stressing over debt? Gone. Gone. Gone! You are shaping the life you want to live.

Here are fourteen steps (in no particular order) to help you define how you want to live:

1. **Focus** on what matters most in your life. Is it your marriage and kids? Your family? Pursuing your passion? Don't forget financial freedom.

2. **Post it**: I AM DEBT-FREE on your computer, refrigerator, and bathroom mirror—any and everywhere until it reads true. And then keep it there to reaffirm your truth!

3. **Brain trash**: Toss it out. All negative thoughts, worrying, what-ifs, whatnots, and could-bes should be eliminated and replaced with inspirational ideas. If you find yourself in the mud, say, "Flip it," and flip-flop that thing you *don't* want into what you *do* want.

4. **Meditate**: As you should with prayer, meditate when you first get up, when your mind is most clear, and focus only on your dream life.

5. **Goals**: Use your smartphone notes, memo, calendar for alerts, or an old-fashioned plume and spiral notepad, whichever is best for you. Make it fun but all relevant to the Cheap Girls Club movement.

   ◊ Short term (Daily, Weekly): Jot down three things you want to be completed per day. If only one or none gets achieved, start again the following day. For instance, add a positive goal, save $1 a day, removing the second cup of caffeine. Reduce something negative: don't buy the morning donut. Maybe take the stairs at work (positive) while eliminating working through lunch (negative).

   ◊ Long term (Monthly, Quarterly, Yearly): Try to erase one bad spending habit per month. Baby steps!

6. **Believe** that your best life is ahead. Even if you've had the greatest day of your life, that night go to bed thinking, *My tomorrows will be even better.*

7. **Pray**: It makes a world of difference. As soon as you open your eyes each morning, thank God for His graces that you are here for another day, and then for the smaller things we all take for granted. (If you're atheist skip to step 8).

8. **Take action**: To see your vision come to fruition, you must act. We have a saying, Be about it. Refer back to those goals and make them happen!

9. **Frown upon basic**: You will not live an average life because you are NOT an average person. If you want to live your dream life, then think and dream big. Grow through life experiences and live in abundance.

10. **Be mindful of what you drink in**: If you're constantly watching and listening to negative programming, or surrounding yourself with those who speak doom and gloom, make concessions. Start small. Take one day off from violent, angry, sad, or depressing programming and peers. Make Sunday a news-free day. I used to watch murder mysteries nearly ten hours a day. At home, at work, the cable channels would be fixed to specific networks. My spirit drank in all that darkness daily. It was all so fascinating—forensics, trace evidence, ballistics. During the day I created, developed, and wrote crime fiction, so it all seemed relevant, but then I realized I had trouble sleeping. I was hyper paranoid. It seemed the killer was always hiding in the closet. Now, I limit television altogether and watch only a few hours a week, which is a tremendous feat. This small change has allowed the light to shine through. Do the same with naysayers and negative friends and family. Limit conversa-

tions if they begin and end with gossip, backbiting, lies, and chaos. And if you're the person who loves to gossip, backbite, lie, and cause chaos, then check yourself.

11. **Have a mantra**: Either self-made or borrowed. Mine has always been "No weapon formed against me shall prosper." Those few words always strengthened me when I most needed to be centered.

12. **Don't tip the boat**: If you are not a morning person, don't set your alarm for 4:30 am and expect to consistently get up to be productive. Stick with your strengths.

13. **Self-Care** is key to living a healthy, advantageous, and fulfilling life. Take time for yourself to meditate, read, connect with nature, and nurture your passions.

14. **Daily Affirmations** are great motivators and also help keep you centered. Jot down some statements to help boost your morale, remind you what's really important, and add some positive energy into your day. Here are my personal affirmations that I've programmed into my smartphone calendar that alerts me each hour.

    ◊ Become what you believe.

    ◊ Be the best you that you could be.

    ◊ Feast or Famine. You decide.

    ◊ You will reap the fruit of your words.

    ◊ Detox. Fast. Meditate.

    ◊ What is it that YOU want?

    ◊ YOLO. So *carpe diem*.

    ◊ Any day above ground is a blessing.

Carve out a life that excites you. Your vision need not be costly or, frankly, cost a dime. There is bountiful enjoyment in nature, state parks, and public beaches. For years, I've lived 160 steps from the beach. The only thing that separates the shoreline and my building is the boardwalk. Summer after summer I found refuge spending money and growing my debt to visit Caribbean islands, looking for something that was right in front of me all along. While I frolicked in the calm blue waters and sandy beaches of Aruba, I frowned upon what was free. It had no value. I took it for granted, as most people do when things are given and not earned. I had to surmise that if I never spent another coin on vacations, I would forever have a "staycation" right under my nose to enjoy.

The other day I got up early and ventured to the beach just before seven in the morning. Fishermen were out, millennials surfed the waves, and joggers and bicyclists were out getting their exercise. I closed my eyes and allowed the sounds of the waves to wash away any worry of looming deadlines or angst, and decluttered my mind. There are cool coffee and organic juice bars, American, Greek, and Eurasian cuisine a few feet away, but I brought my own sand to the beach. I'm a Cheap Girl; that's what we do.

Another thing I've incorporated into my revamped, debt-free, fabulous life again costs little. A pair of shears, homemade weed killer, and sunscreen about sums it up. For me, there is no greater stress reliever than when I am gardening. I get lost for hours planting and pruning and walk back inside the house feeling refreshed, relaxed, and rejuvenated.

Financial freedom can be achieved through discipline, sacrifice, and specific behaviors you implement into your daily routine, but most importantly, it can be fulfilling and life-affirming. Successful people often repeat simple steps to live happier and healthier lives. Don't try to do too much too soon. Everything should be done in moderation and without guilt. Ask yourself, what do you want? Who are you waking up as? Did you purchase that luxury car for yourself or to impress others? Are your weekly manicures and pedicure appointments something you love doing or feel you should do because of others? Strip down and decide how to authentically live your life, and watch the self-awareness flower bloom.

If I, who admittedly got enjoyment from people-pleasing, sought value being all involved in others' lives, spent money to get emotionally high and to hide my insecurities can change, then so can you. I had to decide how I wanted to live and make my vision my reality. I wanted to live debt-free, so I am. How about you?

 Meditative Minutes

Take a few moments and close your eyes to meditate on the life you want. Don't concentrate on what you should do to get it. Just focus on living peacefully, abundantly, happily, and then make your vision your reality.

 Cheap Girls Club Oath

I remember hearing that the hardest thing for a person to do is not to fight, but to walk away from one. The easiest thing is to spend money, earned and unearned. Vow that your spending will be limited to what is essential to living the life you want.

Chapter Nineteen

Rehab: How to Stay Debt-Free

I know, I know, budgets can be restrictive, and now that you're on the road to being debt-free your credit cards are seemingly calling you. What harm could one large purchase do? Well, a lot. **Credit is not the answer; it's a problem.** Look, getting out of debt is no easy feat, so you must reprogram your mind to avoid a relapse. Remember the sleepless nights, stress-filled days, and the angst that being in debt brought forth? Want that again, then have at it. But if you've taken your journey seriously—if you actually want to save more, spend less, and invest in your financial future, then the tips below could help.

Credit is not the answer; it's a problem.

Ten ways to stay debt-free

Accountability

Hopefully a penny saved is a lesson learned for us all. But if you feel unable to keep up the momentum and dedication it takes to remain on your financial freedom path, then find an accountability partner. Someone you trust to hold you accountable in times of weakness, which most could experience. It's a defense mechanism that's free!

Purchase Wisely

Only purchase what you need after careful thought. If you have a partner, purchases should be discussed in depth.

Lifestyle Changes

Adapt your lifestyle to what you've deemed to be important. Downsizing, minimizing, buying used over new, renting vs. owning a home are all choices to help maintain financial independence.

School Debt

School loans are another drain on financial resources. Think community college, scholarships, and grants before you borrow large sums of money on your education.

Credit

Credit cards are optional, not compulsory. Actually, only use your credit cards if you can pay the bill each month and also if by doing so you get perks. For example, the 5% cash back, airline credit, or reward points mentioned in Ways to Save chapter are useful. Credit cards are dangerous and give you a false sense of wealth, so use your discretion when cracking open your wallet. The APR, false sense of funds, and high credit lines are addictive.

Short-Term Goals

Smaller goals, with a *little* reward to celebrate, helps keep you motivated to stay debt-free. With the surplus cash, think about fattening up your savings or saving $500 toward a rainy day fund. Once that goal is met, then double the target.

Long-Term Goals

With all your new money, pencil in some long-term goals. Increase funds for retirement, plan for a much-needed family vacation, or save for an investment property—anything to encourage you to stay out of arrears.

The Why Factor

Keep your objective front and center and have tunnel vision to remain above water. For me, I have a cumulative screenshot of my past debt to act as a reminder on my smartphone. If I see something that I absolutely want, it's retrieved within seconds to help quell any spending thirsts.

Naysayers

Don't care about outside scrutiny. Always remember, you are the treasurer of your life. Don't buckle under peer pressure.

Budget

Choose your budget method wisely. Don't have such a tight, strict budget where you feel strangled, or you may act out.

How you got into debt should have been identified by now. Staying out could be trickier. There should be few arguments on whether we live in a competitive world. My kid is cuter than yours; my house is bigger than yours; my money is longer than yours—but, seriously, who wants to compete with having the largest debt? No one. We're led to believe that women are pitted against each other by outside influences, yet some women take it upon themselves to battle against another for an imaginary crown, and the debt cycle keeps revolving. Financial literacy helps you evolve.

Debt freedom doesn't mean you can't ever book a vacation or buy high-end amenities. It means you do those things *after* you're debt-free, after you've budgeted for your splurge, and only when you can pay for it with cash. Oh, you thought staying out of debt would be easy? Think again. Anything worth pursuing, attaining, and maintaining takes discipline.

 ## Meditative Minutes

Think about how it felt to be enslaved to debt, shackled with overdue bills, and starved of happiness. Then meditate on how wonderful and abundantly fulfilling it is to be debt-free. Freedom from debt is an unequivocally wonderful feeling. Financial freedom is like no other feeling.

 ## Cheap Girls Club Oath

Let's promise to never end up in debt again. Like, ever.

Part 3

Invest

Chapter Twenty

Invest in Your Future

*I*nvesting in your future is insurance against having to work in your golden years, unless you want to. When people hear investments, they instantly think stocks. Yes, that's one way, but there are several ways to invest in your future: stocks, bonds, cash, certificates of deposit, mutual funds, options, exchange-traded funds (ETFs), precious metals, rare coin collection, real estate, your own business, other businesses, or futures.

Whatever the allocated percentage per investment, a proactive approach should begin, like, yesterday. The sooner you start, the better the outcome. You want to make your money generate money? Investing helps your money grow with time (appreciating real estate, rare coin collection, and businesses) and time + interest (stocks, cash accounts, bonds, CDs, ETFs). It's a logical avenue to money expansion and creates wealth.

What's most vital is maximizing your gains and reducing your losses. Where should you invest in to see the most increase? Well, that, my girls, is a YOU decision, but hopefully with the tools in this book, research, and guidance you now know that you should, ultimately, invest. As disclosed in the very beginning of this book, I am not a financial advisor. Nothing in this book is intended to serve as investment or tax advice.

A key component to investing is to have a diverse portfolio[8]. Diversity helps you reach your financial goals while lessening your risks against losses. Diversification[9] harkens back to the don't-put-your-eggs-in-one-basket adage.

While contemplating how to invest your money, stay away from get-rich-quick schemes and other risky investments that promise big bucks in a short amount of time. Odds are, if it seems too good to be true, it isn't true. Remember the pyramid scheme my friend tried to get me to invest in? Yeah, get ghost from those shenanigans.

Mistrustful Saver

My grandmother's generation did not trust banks. She was born in 1915, which predates the 1933 start of the FDIC[10]. During the 1920s and early 1930s, thousands of banks would fail each year. If you had the misfortune of having your money in a failing bank, hopes of stability, home ownership, or a family car would be wiped out. Families began a practice of hiding money under mattresses, in cereal boxes, or in glass jars to keep it safe. The reasoning behind not placing your savings in a bank has not evolved. People are still stashing currency in jars and under mattresses, with a just-in-case-the-sky-falls mentality. But you should know that the money will not generate money, and the odds of that mattress money being enough to sustain you are slim. So think smart. You're not investing in your future. You're investing in an archaic idea of financial security.

---

8   A Portfolio is a group of separate investments/assets either managed directly by you (investor) or managed by a broker, brokerage, or financial advisor.
9   Diversification does not give assurances against losses.
10 Federal Deposit Insurance Corporation, founded June 16, 1933. FDIC limits, as of 2017, is $250,000 per institution.

Old School

You can do it old school and work, place a portion in your savings account, and rely on social security to be your only source of supplemental income. Let's say you retire at 70 to maximize your SSI, and, as an example, you receive $1500/month. Your nest egg of saved income is a healthy $220,000, and your home is paid off. Let's say you live to be 90 years old. To not have more life than you saved for, you must allot $916/month from your savings, leaving you with a combined $2416 per month to live off. Now consider inflation, healthcare, property taxes, utilities, emergencies, food, insurance, maintenance, medication, and you should get anxious. Now let's up the ante. What if we no longer have social security as our supplemental income and you had to live off $916/month? Get the picture? This is the forecast should you only allot for cash investments; low paying interests rates will only get you but so far.

Informed

I had a teacher whose name I've forgotten, but she had wild, frizzy blonde hair, bug eyes, and always wore black. She was a man-hater and would tell us girls to always have your spouse sign a prenup no matter what our pay grade was. She taught Estates, Trusts, and Wills and tried to drill into our heads to invest in a Roth IRA. She wasn't a financial advisor, but she knew if we started young, that we could amass a nice retirement account. She explained that since 1926, 10% was the average annual return in the stock market and that if we invested as little as $1000/annually by the time we retired, we would be millionaires. Forty-five thousand grossing me a million dollars seemed as if she were trying to sell me the Brooklyn Bridge. I was a skeptical twenty year old, and I allowed her financial gem to slip between my fingers. What

I didn't ponder was that she wasn't selling anything because she wasn't gaining anything. She had no agenda other than to get her students on the right financial path early in their lives. I had only to waltz my preoccupied-with-material-things body across the street and speak with

 Time is your best ally, so start early.

a financial advisor, and I would have learned there was truth in her words. Time is your best ally, so start early. I repeat, start early, and demonstrate to your children how to invest early!

It was yet another teachable moment I let slip by. I was informed at a young age, twenty, and I chose to not take heed. This is why I go so hard now, to make up for lost investment years. Cheap Girls, don't be like me. Don't let financial jewels get drowned out by your childlike choices.

The Dumb-Dumb in the Mirror Was Me

Before I became a self-proclaimed cheap girl, I was spendthrift-ing my way through North and South America and Europe. If I had it, I spent it. If I had credit, I spent that too. You only live once motto was in full effect. My past actions were the antithesis of what I now stand for. Retirement saving and planning was so far off to me, I used every excuse to start tomorrow: It doesn't fit into my budget. I'm still young. As soon as I pay off these bills, I'll think about it.

My peers and my neighborhood indoctrinated me into a world of excess. Who did I look up to and how were they living? That was my design. My only mentor with words of financial wisdom was from one lecture, from one teacher, on one day of my life. And it just wasn't enough to break the cycle.

This did it for me. Years later the chatter started about social security running out. The hysteria swelled as the likelihood made the headlines and economists predicted that the till would be depleted right around the time I would be eligible. Say what now? How is this fair? But we all know (say it with me) that life isn't fair, so suck it up and make provisions. Deal with it.

Finally, I sat down with a financial advisor. He had on a suit, family pictures on his desk, and began by running down his resume of all the well-known firms he had worked for before ultimately settling for this brokerage company. He asked questions about age, employment, and gross income, planted my money into preset funds, and sent me on my way.

Back then, it wasn't that I didn't ask the right questions; I asked *no questions*. The reason he had chosen a particular fund to park my money into wasn't explained, because he didn't have to win my business. He knew that whether he said little or a lot, it would not change the outcome. I was an inexperienced investor, and within thirty minutes he would be on to the next one.

The next year, I arrived with another check—the max the IRS allowed me to invest toward retirement. This repetitive action was what I did with little **Life isn't fair, so suck it up and make provisions.** thought. Statements came, or they didn't. I would never know because I wasn't focused on retirement. Folks said I should do it, so I finally did. Truthfully, I do not remember the amount of money that I initially invested with this broker. What I learned later, after finally taking an interest in my money and how it was being spent, was the high fees were eating away at my bottom line.

It's debatable whether you should have managed or unmanaged trades. There are lower fees with unmanaged accounts because there is less buying and selling involved. However, portfolios should be rebalanced. Mine was actively managed, which meant that the broker could sell my investments from one fund to another. Each time he made a trade, he received a fee. My portfolio also had high "hidden" operating fees. Although one would argue that fees aren't hidden because they are listed in the Prospectus[11], it is unknown until the broker, or statements make it so. Not once did he ever mention "fees."

Fast-forward to post-2008. People were losing their homes by the thousands, stocks took a nosedive, and American families needed relief from our government—and let's not forget the bailouts for the banking industry. Everyone's nerves were frayed.

I went to sit down with my same financial advisor guy—sidebar: a cutie by the way. But I digress. For the first time, I had a host of questions. I had substantial money to place into my pension, and I was nervous. So I began asking questions, and I will never forget how his eyes widened. He was bewildered and thrown off guard. As he evaded my questions, I would redirect him to seek clarification. He shifted in his seat several times, readjusted his rolled-up sleeves, and kept looking past me when he spoke. Finally, he said he would have to get back with me to follow up.

He waited a couple weeks before he called. I sat back down with him and waited for answers. When none came, I realized he was a one-trick pony. I never left that check.

I decided to explore my options, so I went to appointment after appointment and heard the same spiels from different people. They would place 80% of my income into Fund A and 20% into Fund

11 Prospectus is filed with the SEC (Security and Exchange Commission) and details a publicly traded company.

B. Because of my age that was so. Period. If I winced at 80/20, they would quickly recover and say, "OK, no problem. 70/30 works best for you! Still, uncomfortable? Then we can adjust." None of those plans was tailored specifically for me because it wasn't about me. One

> **When someone has something to gain from you, your needs will always be secondary.**

hundred thousand people could walk in and the only difference would be the percentage, not the fund. These advisors weren't my friends and could not care less than two tears in a bucket about my financial future. Whenever someone has something to gain from you, your needs will always be secondary. Whether it's a percentage, bonus, or flat fee, an agenda is built into the advice that's given.

In conclusion, the "why" could never be answered. It seemed as though everyone had gone to the same seminar, studied the same materials, and got hired to fill the same positions. But could these people make me money? And if the "why" was simple—because the fund has performed well in the past—then so be it. I kept thinking there was more. These advisors claimed to have a bullet-proof plan to help me make money, but I realized there are no guarantees in investing.

The next foolish but cautionary thing I did for the next few years was place my pension into low-interest bearing certificates of deposits. I had to play it safe until I could summon up the gumption to become my own financial advisor and make my own trades. The "safe" play garnered me .02% in compound interest[12] in CDs that matured quarterly. Please don't laugh, although I am laughing. I tell you, sometimes my actions crack me up. I was aware enough not to sink my pension into long-term commitments because I knew that

---

12 Compound Interest is when the interest on the interest of the principal is reinvested and not paid out.

eventually I would roll the pension into investments, but meanwhile, the certificates of deposits would serve as placeholders.

The chart below demonstrates the growth of the recommended $1000 by my teacher had I made only a one-time investment and then quit. For example, I will use the rate of growth of my previous CDs (.02%), long-term CDs at the current rate of (2%), and average stock market return (10%) per the 1926 data.

Compound Interest: Same investment. Different results.

YEAR	0.02%	2%	10%
1	1,000.20	1,020.00	1,100.00
5	1,001.00	1,104.08	1,610.51
15	1,003.00	1,345.87	4,177.25
25	1,005.01	1,640.61	10,834.71

You can see from the chart I played it safe. My CDs were FDIC insured. Therefore my investment was no-risk. However what I was essentially doing was allowing the institution I had sunken my money into, virtually, to have an almost interest-free loan. Do you know what they do with your money held in CDs? They invest it in the stock market. So while I was getting a paltry 0.02% return on my investment (ROI), the company was averaging 10%. Did I know this going in? Sadly, yes. But I allowed my fear to do all the decision-making.

Does the stock market fluctuate and crash? It does. You have only to turn on any local news channel, peruse the stock market on your smartphone, or chitchat with an avid investor to know this. But it's wise to invest in something. You've read my Dear Abby letter, and it's filled with enough mistakes to fill this book. Yet I survived. I am thriving financially and still growing. The message is to invest—NOT what to invest in. That's your job. Today there are enough tools at your fingertips to arm you with the knowledge and confidence you need.

Get into the Right Investment Headspace:

1. Know that the larger the gain (return), the riskier the investment.
2. Know that the market fluctuates and even crashes, but if you keep your money in for the long haul, you should still see growth.
3. Know your tolerance risk level and take the surveys to find out what that may be. (Conservative, Balanced, Growth, Aggressive)
4. Know that the sooner you invest, the larger your gains (compound interest) will be at retirement time.
5. Know that you should speak with a financial advisor or planner, but you don't HAVE to do so.
6. Know that you can be your own financial advisor and make your own trades (see below).

Risk Tolerance Quizzes:

◊ http://www.individual.ml.com/?id=15261_45434
◊ https://www.calcxml.com/calculators/inv08
◊ https://njaes.rutgers.edu/money/riskquiz/
◊ https://www.newyorklife.com/learn-and-plan/risk-tolerance-calculator

Some Online Brokerages For Trades:

◊ E*Trade
◊ TD Ameritrade
◊ Fidelity
◊ Ally
◊ Merrill Edge
◊ Charles Schwab

When to Invest:

Debt first

This book is broken into three sections (save more, spend less, and then invest) for a reason. **Pay off debt before you make any investments.** That's because it's a numbers game. If the ten-year average ROI is 10% (example) and your credit card debt accrues at 13-29% with minimal payments you are hustling backward. **Compound interest works both ways.**

Early

As soon as you have more than two nickels to rub together you should think about throwing your hat into the investment arena. The earliest in reaps the most benefits.

White noise

Try not to listen to those market analyzers who study market trends to gauge if an investor could make the most money. However the market fluctuates, you should first get in.

Be mindful, not watchful

You've heard, "A watched pot never boils." Well, checking on your investments minute by minute isn't necessary, but just don't walk away and come back a year later to assess what's gone on. I review mine once a week, but you could do monthly or quarterly. Do what works best to keep you informed.

Rebalance

Before you invest you should have a target portfolio that outlines what percentage you should have allocated considering your age or risk level. At some point, you may need to rebalance your portfolio (buy and sell shares).

Below are a couple of sites with great Asset Allocation Calculators.

◊ Bankrate.com

◊ TRowePrice.com

Financial advisors, as any profession, are like mechanics—not all of them are good. So with that, I used my own noggin to invest the largest chunk of my retirement. However, my early investments are still actively and non-actively managed by brokerage firms. I also have cash accounts and real estate investments. This was best for me. Find your investing muscle and strengthen it over time. This has been a journey for me, not a sprint. And remember, before I stepped outside the box to trade, there were years when I went with the safest play, and that was OK because it all falls under the umbrella of learning growth.

What if you don't want to use a financial advisor to handle your investments, yet you aren't confident enough to do your own trading? A robo-advisor is an automated investment service where a computer algorithm manages your investment portfolio with minimal human intervention. Robo-advisors have features such as tax-loss harvesting and automated portfolio rebalancing at a lower cost. This service can translate to lower fees and larger net profits for the investor.

Overall, below are some robo-advisors that you could look into on your journey. Do your due diligence before making any investment decisions. Look for any promotions, management fees, and account minimums. The literature on these advisors is relatively new, dating back about five years. You will find pros and cons arguments on how effective these services are, so use your best judgment.

Management for a Fee

◊ Betterment.com

◊ Wealthfront.com

◊ TDAmeritrade.com

◊ FidelityGo.com

Fee-Free Management

◊ CharlesSchwab.com

◊ WiseBanyan.com

Hybrids – Robo and Financial Advisor

◊ Vanguard.com

◊ CharlesSchwab.com

Taxable Accounts

◊ Wealthfront.com

◊ PersonalCapital.com

401(k) Management:

◊ Blooom.com (requires subscription fee)

 Meditative Minutes

Visualize your money growing to heights you never thought possible.

 Cheap Girls Club Oath

We invest in depreciating assets, we invest in relationships, and we invest in other people. Take an oath to invest in yourself and in your future.

Chapter Twenty-One

Tax-Deferred, Tax-Free, and Taxable Accounts! Oh My!

Now that you've lowered your car insurance, gotten rid of that hefty cable bill, and turned a hobby into some serious cash flow, what are you going to do with all your savings? Well, the former you might want to blow it on a new sofa, a pair of "red bottoms," or a vehicle upgrade. No chance of that. The frugal new you will dump that extra cash into your retirement. Here's the thing—you were paying it out anyway, so you shouldn't feel the pinch.

So here we are, almost at the end of our financial fierceness Cheap Girls Club journey. I hope the thought of investing has become a priority. Theoretically, waiting five years could cost you tens of thousands; ten years, hundreds of thousands. It's not a hard rule, but every ten years your investment doubles. To belabor the point, I need you to understand that **each year, each investment dollar counts**! An essential part of financial literacy is getting familiar with the different retirement plans. Carve out time—a weekend or a couple of weeks—to get a full understanding of any retirement-related decisions.

Everyone should prioritize retirement investing but, (1) people in low-income neighborhoods, (2) people with low-paying salaries, (3) independent contractors, (4) civil servants, (5) self-employed, and (6) college students should specifically seize the opportunity because there is one, should you map it out. I know it's hard sometimes making ends meet when you're barely keeping your head above water. But with aggressively finding ways to save and earn you could make consistent contributions.

I lived in public housing and tenement buildings as a youth, and when I would stare out my window, all I would see was poverty and lack. There was love there and a sense of community—lifelong friends and even loyalty. But financial education and investing was off topic. That was some time ago, and thankfully conversations have elevated to include money awareness.

Let us focus for a moment on those who could benefit most from getting in early so we could get out of poverty. Cash-based businesses such as the nail technician, dancer (traditional or exotic), video vixen, waitress, hair stylist, or starving artist all should make a contribution to a retirement fund.

People in low-income neighborhoods with low-paying salaries must prioritize investing. Our latter half of life could be so much better than our humble beginnings. We find money for pampering ourselves, expensive grooming such as makeup, weaves, hair extensions, designer clothing, and whatnots.

Each year, each investment dollar counts! Reallocate those funds toward building your future and getting out. If in my early teens financial literacy was discussed at the dinner table—if we had dinner at the table—then when my college professor discussed retirement planning with her students, perhaps I would have known to get in at that moment.

Besides my self-funded retirement investments, I have a small pension from a government job. Government jobs, city and state, have great retirement plans. Plan, budget, and strategize to live a healthy, wealthy and vibrant life.

I know it's challenging looking thirty-forty years into your future. But if you do, then you could retire with a sweet retirement nest egg. Living in the moment has its allure. To assign present finances toward future retirement earnings is achievable, and you will adjust to living with a portion of your income allotted for investments. Whether your retirement is self-funded or employer-funded, aim to get in, and you shall win. Be ambitious! Don't walk in the shadows of debt and a future of uncertainty.

When you're twenty, you may look at someone forty or fifty and think they're almost dead, but before you know it, you will be there too. Get yourself into a long-term investment vehicle and hit the accelerator.

Take A Moment To Get Familiar With The Different Plans Via The Internal Revenue Service.[13]

◊   https://www.irs.gov/retirement-plans

Depending on the chosen retirement plan, either the employer or employee chooses the investment fund.

Types of Retirement Accounts

401(k)

Usually offered by an employer. This retirement plan allows you to invest pre-tax[14] dollars, enable it to grow, and you are only **taxed**

---

13   Check with the IRS, a tax advisor or planner for contribution deadlines per plan.
14   You haven't paid taxes on this income, yet.

when you withdraw at retirement. A misconception is this is a tax-free retirement fund, which it is not. You can have taxable investment accounts where taxes are paid NOW (the year of the investment) or tax-deferred investment accounts where you are taxed LATER at the time of withdrawal.

◊ Your tax-deferred income gets compounded until withdrawal when you are taxed.

◊ There's a 10% penalty if you withdraw funds early, before **59 ½**, and any income taxes due.

◊ The IRS has a short list of rules that may qualify you for a penalty-free withdrawal. Before you withdraw, consult the IRS website or a tax advisor.

◊ There are limitations to what you can invest. For 2017, it's $18,000 annually.

◊ Your employer has a wealth of information on these plans. Opening one is easy-peasy. Go to your Human Resources department and get the ball rolling.

◊ If offered, take full advantage if your employer matches your contribution. **A 401(k) match is FREE MONEY**, something us Cheap Girls should gravitate toward. Basically, if the 401(k) match from your employer is $5000 annually, then they will match each dollar you invest up to that $5000 cap. Focus on the free money and get the **full company match**. Don't leave money on the table. I cannot stress this enough!

◊ Set-up automatic deductions to simplify the process.

Roth 401(k)

Usually offered by an employer. Roth 401(k) contributions are monies invested into your plan with your post-taxed dollars. Taxes are taken up front, at the time of investment, and not at retirement withdrawal. Your gains grow tax-free.

◊ At age 70 ½ you must take a percentage of mandatory withdrawals.

◊ You are penalized if you do not take withdrawals after the mandatory age of 70 ½.

◊ The maximum contribution you can make for 2017 is $18,000. Age 50 and over, $24,000. $18,000 plus an additional $6,000 to catch up.

◊ There are no income restrictions for eligibility.

◊ There is a five-year limitation for withdrawals from the date of conversion.

◊ You **ARE** penalized if you make withdrawals before 59 ½.

◊ Consult the Internal Revenue Service website or your tax advisor for additional details.

If you're like me, you have allowed or are allowing an excellent opportunity to go to waste. Before I had to fund my own retirement, I could have invested in a 401(k) where my employer would match my contribution 100% up to a certain amount per year. Not to make excuses, but in my early twenties, I passed on a great financial opportunity because all these plans were insanely difficult to understand. It was easier to ignore them even though I knew they were in my best interest.

Roth IRA (Individual Retirement Account):

A Roth IRA is straightforward. These retirement accounts are traditionally recommended to people in their 20s, but are great at any age. Roth IRA contributions are monies invested into your plan with your post-taxed dollars. Taxes are taken up front, at the time of investment, and not at retirement withdrawal. Roth IRAs are great plans should you qualify. Basically, your gains grow tax-free.

◊ Taxed income is placed into mutual funds, ETFs, stocks, bonds, whichever is chosen for your Roth IRA, **and you are not taxed later when**

you withdraw for retirement.

◊ The maximum contribution you can make for 2017 is $5500. Age 50 and over, $6500.

◊ There are income restrictions for eligibility. For 2017 for single filers with a modified Adjusted Gross Income (AGI) is phased out with income between $118,000 and $133,000 and $186,000 and $196,000 for married couples.

◊ NO age restriction.

◊ There is a five-year limitation for withdrawals from the date of conversion.

◊ You are not penalized if you withdraw your principal investment.

◊ You **ARE** penalized if you withdraw your investment earnings, the gains before 59 ½.

◊ There are qualifying reasons to make a penalty-free withdrawal. Consult the Internal Revenue Service website or your tax advisor for exceptions to these rules.

Traditional IRA

A traditional IRA retirement plan is tax-deductible (state and federal) per contribution year. However, income taxes are due at the time of your withdrawal.

◊ Age restriction, 70 ½ for earned income contributions.

◊ At age 70 ½ you must take a percentage of mandatory taxable withdrawals.

◊ The maximum contribution you can make for 2017 is $5500. Age 50 and over, $6500.

◊ There aren't any income restrictions.

◊ At age 59 ½ you can take withdrawals without penalty.

◊ Contributions made during the contribution tax year lowers your taxable income. This may place you in a lower tax bracket, allowing you to get additional tax incentives. Consult the Internal Revenue Service website or a tax advisor for additional details.

◊ You **ARE** penalized 10% of the amount withdrawn before 59 ½.

So let's quickly compare the Roth IRA vs. traditional IRA. Which do you choose? Most financial advisors like the Roth, but it's your decision. Basically, it's a guessing game. You must decide whether you think your taxable income is higher now, or later when you retire. The tax rate you pay on your Roth IRA now will be greater or less than the tax rate you'll pay on your traditional IRA withdrawals later. How can anyone predict this? Most economists concluded that our tax rates are historically low and because our national deficit is exorbitant, taxes will only rise. Perhaps this makes the Roth IRA a better choice. You'll have to research what tax bracket you're in and ask yourself what your career trajectory is. Are you expecting to make higher income closer to your retirement? Or are you in your prime earning years? That, my girls, is the question.

NOW & LATER	
NOW	LATER
Taxable	**Tax-Deferred**
Roth 401(k)	401(k)
Roth IRA	Traditional IRA
	SIMPLE IRA
	SEP IRA

Employees, Self-Employed, Small Business Owners

SIMPLE and SEP IRAs are seemingly similar. However, distinct differences should be noted.

Simple IRA

Savings Incentive Match Plan for Employees helps small employers with 100 or fewer employees (and themselves) with a simplified retirement plan. The employee may elect to make income-reducing contributions. Matched or nonelective contributions are required by the employer. This retirement plan allows the employee to invest pre-tax[15] dollars, enable it to grow, and are only **taxed when monies are taken out at retirement.**

◊ If within the first two years of joining the plan you make an early withdrawal, there's a 25% penalty before age **59 ½**, and any income taxes due.

◊ After that, there's a 10% penalty if you withdraw funds early, before **59 ½**, and any income taxes due.

◊ Consult the Internal Revenue Service website or a tax advisor for additional information.

◊ Employer contributions are tax-deductible.

◊ Employees' tax-deferred income gets compounded until withdrawal when you are taxed.

◊ Employee:

◊ Contribution limits for 2017 is $12,500. If aged 50 or older by December 31st, the contribution limit is $15,500.

◊ Employer:

---

15   You haven't paid taxes on this income yet.

◊ Option A requires the employer to match the employee's contribution up to 3%. Should an employer elect to contribute less than 3%, then the employee must be notified before the 60-day election period of that calendar year. The employer's contribution can be no less than 1% for two years out of a five-year time frame.

◊ Option B. The nonelective contribution is 2% for all employees that are eligible. Under this option, the employee can elect to not make contributions to his/her SIMPLE IRA retirement plan. However, the employer must still contribute 2% of the employee's annual income. Should an employer elect this contribution method, the employee must be notified before the 60-day election period of that calendar year.

◊ For 2017, the IRA has the eligibility compensation at $270,000.

SEP IRA

Simplified Employee Pension allows the employer or self-employed individual to make contributions for themselves as well as toward their employee's retirement plan. This retirement plan allows you to invest pre-tax dollars and is only **taxed when you take it out at retirement.**

◊ There's a 10% penalty if you withdraw funds early, before **59 ½**, and any income taxes due.

◊ This retirement plan cannot go above the lesser of 25% of the employee's income, or $54,000 for 2017.

◊ All contributions are solely employer funded.

◊ Consult the Internal Revenue Service website or a tax advisor for additional information.

Meditative Minutes

As we age, we respect the advice our parents gave us. What if that guidance didn't include our finances? You started late or not at all and you want to beat yourself up with guilt. Please don't. Learn from the past, live in the present, and prepare for your future. Meditate on now and later.

Cheap Girls Club Oath

Take an oath to either make an appointment with your Human Resources department, financial advisor or planner, or schedule ME TIME to kickstart your retirement planning.

Chapter Twenty-Two

Adjournment

We've come a long way, and we're still not done. The end game has always been financial awareness. Cheap Girls Club is much bigger than just being cheap. Cheap is the foundation to build your infrastructure upon. I hope you gleaned that from this book. The Cheap Girls Club is a sisterhood of women who now refuse to part with their money on nouns: people, places, and things—until they've ruminated on debt vs. asset, needs vs. wants, essentials vs. nonessentials.

In order to sleep peacefully at night you can't squander your money on parasites who benefit from your hard-earned dollars and then would rather choke on the words "thank you" before allowing them to spill from their mouths. Our inner financier should be awakened, and we should recognize the downside of investing in depreciable assets, overspending on essentials, and splurging on nonessentials. You should now be a cautious, informed spender who has a deep respect for money. Your fear of investing should be minimized, if not eradicated, when you think about all the money you've pissed away throughout the years.

Hard rule: Feeling obligated or pressured to loan someone money? Don't. Consider dumping it into a (small, medium, or large cap) stock instead—anywhere besides ungrateful pockets.

You should know now that being selfish isn't a shame-inducing label, and being called *cheap* should be worn as a badge of honor. "Yes, I am" should be your reply.

 ## Meditative Minutes

Meditate on the knowledge you've gained about yourself and your relationship with money.

 ## Cheap Girls Club Oath

In conclusion, take an oath to stay CHEAP, girls! Meeting adjourned.

#CheapGirlsClubChallenge

Here are the parameters for those who are committed and have taken the rules of the Cheap Girls Club seriously. Challenge yourself to …

Save More

1. **I pledge to save more by:** _____.
   a. Cutting cable costs
   b. Lowering utility bills
   c. Defensive driving deduction
   d. Dining in
   e. Transferring high credit card debt to lower APR introductory rates
   f. Shopping for necessities through reward based websites
   g. Shopping in discount clothing outlets
   h. Thrift store buying
   i. Using tax-software
   j. Lowering any/all insurances
   k. Multi-meal planning
   l. Container gardens
   m. Groupon deals for social activities
   n. Cost-free hobbies
   o. All the above
   p. Other: _____

2. **Jot down up to five talents that you can monetize.**
   a. _____
   b. _____
   c. _____
   d. _____
   e. _____

3. I have found additional ways to earn by:

_____

4. Monthly, I am on track to save approximately:_____.
  a. $25 - $150
  b. $150 - $300
  c. $300 - $500
  d. $500 or greater

5. My annual financial savings goal for (enter year) _____ is:
  a. $1000
  b. $2500
  c. $5000
  d. Other: _____

Spend Less

1. My spending trigger(s) are: _____.
  a. Stress
  b. Good news
  c. Social media
  d. Holidays
  e. People pleasing
  f. Shopping
  g. Depression
  h. Credit cards
  i. Image
  j. Subterfuge
  k. Gambling
  l. All the above
  m. Other: _____.

2. I have gone _____ without vanity shopping for unnecessary nonessentials.

    a. One week

    b. One month

    c. Three months

    d. Six months

    e. One-year is the GOAL

3. I have taken an oath to say no to: _____.

    a. Lending money

    b. Wedding participation

    c. Being a godparent

    d. Attending children's parties when I have none

    e. Favors

    f. Getting credit in my name for others

    g. Allowing houseguests to move in rent free

    h. Giving out advice

    i. Giving away my free time

    j. Work-related, pressured purchases

    k. Girl Scout cookies

    l. All the above

    m. Other: _____

Invest

1. I vow to join a retirement plan _____.

    a. Monday

    b. The 1st of the month

    c. The first day of the new year

Benchmark

◊ Your accomplishments
◊ Your progress
◊ Your growth

FINANCIAL GOAL	DATE
I have found ways to save.	
I have found ways to earn.	
I have created a budget.	
I have made my emergency savings goal.	
I have chosen and begun a debt repayment plan.	
I am debt-free.	
I have set up my investment portfolio.	
I have not made my goal. Today I begin again. *	

* Situations may arise that we cannot foresee. Should you not meet your goal for any reason, don't give up. Begin again.

Just Say No List

- Lending money
- Wedding participation
- Being a godparent
- Attending children's parties when I have none
- Favors
- Getting credit in my name for others
- Allowing houseguests to move in rent free
- Giving out advice
- Giving away my free time
- Work-related, pressured purchases
- Girl Scout cookies

Post These Everywhere!

Acknowledgments

God gets all the glory. He is forever present in my thoughts and actions. Regardless of how many tribulations I go through, I seek Him first. Most of my life I have been searching for Eden. A sanctuary where I could feel safe. Growing up with an epicenter of violence just steps from your door you could walk either way; toward darkness or the light. I have experienced both, and I know how I want to live my life.

Daddy, one hundred forty-two months just wasn't enough. Until I see you again, sleep peacefully. Your laughter could light up a room, and I've missed you since the first day you departed.

My whole foundation rests upon the strong shoulders of Callie Bell Battle. She believed I could. Therefore, I am. My grandmother taught me the power of prayer, the key to meditation, to fight for equality, and to allow no one to make me feel less than. I can still hear her voice asking me to repeat, *je m'appelle,* Crystal. Regretfully, I never learned French, but it's on my bucket list.

Katrice Ashley, Dylan Bella, and Brooke-Lynn Quinn—my three girls! If I were a mom, you three kiddos are the perfect daughters. Honored, blessed, and grateful for you beauties. Moreover, to Treece, who allowed me to co-parent her child during summers to exercise my mommy muscle, only to finally conclude what I already knew was true: I am not Mommy Material. *Sigh.*

My Winslow, Shim, and Battle family—with love, always!

Jimmy, my Irishman. You always find the funny in any situation. You are witty, intelligent, and have inspired me for quite some time. You rarely miss my birthday, and each year my born day is that much more special when I receive your beautiful bouquet of roses. You took in my fur babies (Cody and Lulu) when they needed a good home and loved them throughout their years. We are more alike than not, and whether you know it or not, you have taught me to care about those who care about me. We go way back, and I love and respect you. Thanks for your legal two cents, being a good listener, and remaining a loyal friend.

Candace, you have the kindest heart. I trust you, and I do not trust many. I am so privileged to work with you and to call you my friend and confidante. It is so rare to come across someone with so many talents, who undoubtedly and sincerely wants to see me win. With you, there isn't an agenda! You're authentic and priceless to me.

To the person who should appreciate being nameless. Your friendship, guidance, strength, and loyalty are unquantifiable. You're special because you were there through good and crazy times, and my heart will always have a place with you in it. You're my dude. Always! I. Love. You. Words never spoken, but no less true.

I have neighbors, the Carolls, eighty and eighty-one years young, who are always baking me coconut cakes and sending over fig preserves. The smiles on their faces is endearing, and I cannot stop squeezing them with tight hugs. They will never read this book, or even know of its existence, but it makes me feel good sharing their beautiful hearts with the world.

Frenemies and enemies, situations solved, and problems dissolved, I say this with gratitude—thank you! Thank you for making the good days taste that much sweeter.

There will be individuals who will open this book only to hate it, or hate it without even opening it. I pray for my enemies to place their energy elsewhere besides wasting it on me. I pray for your happiness and fulfillment, because a genuinely happy person doesn't have room enough in their heart to hate.

To those friends who offer kind words and encouragement, who support me from afar and inspired me to keep writing—many, many, thanks!

Hungry for More?
Join the *Club!*